Successful Teaching Practice

in the Lifelong Learning Sector

Vicky Duckworth, Jane Wood,
John Dickinson and John Bostock

LearningMatters

First published in 2010 by Learning Matters Ltd

British Library Cataloguing in Publication Data
A CIP record for this book is available from the British Library.

ISBN: 978 1 84445 350 4

Cover design by Topics – The Creative Partnership
Project management by Deer Park Productions, Tavistock, Devon
Typeset by PDQ Typesetting Ltd, Newcastle under Lyme
Printed and bound in Great Britain by Cromwell Press Group, Trowbridge, Wiltshire

Learning Matters
33 Southernhay East
Exeter EX1 1NX
Tel: 01392 215560
info@learningmatters.co.uk
www.learningmatters.co.uk

Successful Teaching Practice

in the Lifelong Learning Sector

Contents

Dedication

We would like to dedicate this book to our children and families for their unstinting love and support and to our trainees for inspiring us to write the book in the first place.

Acknowledgements

We would like to thank David Ryan for all his help and support.

We would also like to thank the following trainees for their contributions:

Graham Burrill
Kevin Callaghan
Melany Cook
Angela Court-Jackson
Aimie Disley
Andrew George
Chris Jones
Dawn McCone
Lorraine Roberts
Nicola Thornton
Andrew Whittle
George Woodall

Thanks to the following Edge Hill University Staff:

Jacqui Howe
Ray Dwerryhouse

Thanks to:

Amy Thornton at Learning Matters and Jennifer Clark.

The Authors

Vicky Duckworth is Course Leader for the full-time programme in Post-Compulsory Education and Training at Edge Hill University. She is also Research Associate at the Centre for Learning Identity Studies. She is passionate about the empowering and transforming nature of education and keen to establish and maintain strong and productive links between research and practice.

Jane Wood is Course Leader for Professional Development in Post-Compulsory Education and Training at Edge Hill University. Jane has 20 years' experience of teaching vocational courses in further education colleges and has recently worked as curriculum quality manager responsible for raising standards of teaching and learning, and conducting professional observations. Further to this she has managed successful teacher education provision prior to her move to the university.

John Dickinson graduated from Loughborough University of Technology in 1980 and began a career as a residential social worker. In 1982 he joined Kirkby College of Further Education on Merseyside. He taught child care, health and social care and A Level and GCSE psychology. In 1990 his involvement in teacher training for FE staff began. At the last count he had undertaken over 450 lesson observations, from accountancy to zoology and all points in between. John was Chief Examiner for GCSE psychology with SEG between 1995 and 2002. In 2005 he left what had become Knowsley Community College, where he had been Head of Department and Course Leader for the Post-16 Cert. Ed., to join Edge Hill as Senior Lecturer and original member of the Post-compulsory Education and Training Team.

John Bostock is Senior Lecturer in PCET, Course Leader (PDP), and Co-ordinator of mentoring in PCET, Research Nurture Group Convenor, Fellow of the Institute for Learning (IfL) and an Institutional Learning and Teaching Fellow at Edge Hill University. John currently delivers on the Cert. HE/PGCE (PCET), and has also developed and delivered modules for the MA in Education (14–19). John has 20 years' experience of teaching and managing in FE and is an active doctoral researcher in the field of Post-Compulsory Education and Training. Mentoring in PCET, Learning and Teaching Theory particularly, Flexible and E-pedagogy are areas of special interest and John has presented these topics at conferences and workshops.

Introduction

As is the way with teachers everywhere, we were sitting having coffee in the staff room one day, discussing our trainees and how they were getting on with the programme. We were lamenting the lack of accessible textbooks for the trainees to use while they were on their teaching practice to support them in our absence.

As a result of this we came up with the idea of this book and the rest is history.

We were determined to produce a book that could be read as easily by a vocational trainee teaching construction and a trainee teaching A level psychology. The rationale behind the book was to provide support during the assessed teaching when we as tutors would not be available and the mentors might be too busy to provide.

We envisage the book being a simple source of reference and a guide to assist trainee or new teachers, whether they are in-service or pre-service, to undertake their duties with confidence and pride.

The chapters aim to provide a journey through the teaching experience from induction to applying for jobs or moving on within organisations.

It has been a collaboration between colleagues and has been influenced every step of the way by the experiences of the many trainee teachers we teach, observe, tutor and support in our jobs as senior lecturers at Edge Hill University.

We hope that you will find it a useful text and a credible support in developing your teaching practice and in enabling you to succeed on the programme on which you have embarked or may be thinking about taking.

We wish you the very best of luck and hope that you succeed in a career that is not just a job but a vocation that you will enjoy for the rest of your lives.

Jane Wood, Vicky Duckworth, John Bostock and John Dickinson
January 2010

1
Starting your assessed teaching modules

The objectives of this chapter

This chapter has been designed to offer you an insight into researching the organisation in which you are employed or, if you are pre-service, the site of your teaching placement. Further to this it provides key information on the important factors to consider on your induction which include practical issues such as your timetables, health and safety, and the roles and responsibilities of the key players at your organisation. To support your professional development, information related to effectively understanding and organising your teaching file is explored while taking into account key legislation and initiatives.

It addresses the following numbered professional practice standards for QTLS (Qualified Teacher Learning and Skills):

AK 6.1 Relevant statutory requirements and codes of practice for understanding your own role, in relation to responsibilities and boundaries.

AK 6.2 Ways to apply relevant statutory requirements and the underpinning principles.

AK 7.1 Organisational systems and processes for recording learner information.

BK 3.5 Systems for communication within own organisation.

BK 4.1 Good practice in meeting the needs of learners in collaboration with colleagues.

FK 4.2 Processes for liaison with colleagues and other professionals to provide effective guidance and support for learners.

Introduction

The mind is not a vessel to be filled, but a fire to be ignited.

Plutarch

Some of you may have gained experience of the post-compulsory sector as students in a college of further education and/or sixth form. From that initial step into the Lifelong Learning Sector (LLS) the motivation for returning to the sector to teach will vary.

A number of trainee teachers cite a key reason as aspiring to emulate a teacher who has inspired them on their learning journey. Jenny, a former trainee teacher specialising in literacy, recalls:

> *There were those teachers I came across that just weren't interested. It's like they went through the motions but their heart wasn't in it. There was this one teacher, though, Mr Bennett. He really made each lesson full of life and interesting. He made sure everyone was encouraged to play a part in the lesson no matter what their ability. That's probably why I did so well in sociology – he was inspirational. Coming into teaching I wanted to create the buzz he did and make a difference to the lives of those I teach.*

Yvon Appleby's research on adult learners who had joined Skills for Life classes (2004) found that *relationships with the tutor (or volunteer), and with other members of the class or support networks, are important to learners*. Gravells and Simpson (2008) identified teachers as the *most effective resources available to learners* (p61).

As such, teachers can influence whether learning is a positive or not so positive experience for the student. Whereas for some students their progress into Post-Compulsory Education and Training (PCET) is a smooth one, other learners often have to overcome significant barriers to gain the confidence and courage to return to learning, in some cases bringing with them *fear of violence, threat and intimidation* (Barton et al, 2007, p65).

As teachers in PCET you can create a safe learning environment, based on respect, where students can flourish and reach their potential.

Researching your organisation

For those of you who are 'pre-service', you may not be aware of the institutional structures within which you will be working. For those of you already working in the sector you may already have an insight into how these structures promote the quality of teaching and function to facilitate the smooth and effective running of the organisation.

In order to have an insight into the way your organisation is shaped and operates, a good step forward is to familiarise yourself with their 'mission statement'. The mission statement is usually a short written statement of your organisation's vision, goals and philosophies.

Mission statements can be brief, for example:

> *This College will transform lives by offering first class education and training in order to improve employability and generate economic prosperity.*

Or much longer, such as:

> *This college offers a high quality education. All learners are actively encouraged to acquire values and knowledge and to develop pleasures in learning for a lifetime of fulfillment and success. The college promotes an environment of mutual respect where all members of the community are equally valued and work together in an atmosphere of tolerance.*
>
> The college aims
>
> * *To encourage in all high expectations and high standards.*
> * *To promote tolerance and respect for all cultures represented in the college.*
> * *To provide a caring environment within which each learner is valued and is able to develop to their full potential.*
> * *To provide a curriculum and quality of teaching which fosters an enjoyment of learning and develops skills for life.*
> * *To develop in learners a deeper understanding of themselves and to enable them to become responsible citizens with a social, cultural, economic and political awareness.*

REFLECTIVE TASK

REFLECTIVE TASK

1. What is the driving force in the first mission statement?
2. How does the second mission statement differ?

PRACTICAL TASK PRACTICAL TASK PRACTICAL TASK PRACTICAL TASK PRACTICAL TASK

Now research the mission statement in your organisation:
1. What is its vision?
2. What is its ethos?
3. How does this fit into you own vision and ethos?

CASE STUDY

A specialist in art and design, Kathy gives her views on her college's mission statement.

The mission statement at my placement focused on meeting the needs of all the learners no matter what level they arrived at the college. I thought this was really important because it sent out the message that everyone, no matter whether they have a handful of qualifications or none at all, should be offered the opportunity to reach their potential. As someone who left school with no qualifications, only to gain them as a mature student, I wanted other people to have the same chance – the college's mission statement reflected this.

Understanding the roles and responsibilities of all the key players

While teaching in an organisation you will meet and work alongside different staff with differing roles and responsibilities. It is vital that you develop the ability to work within a multidisciplinary team through effective use of a combination of skills, theory, and techniques.

REFLECTIVE TASK

REFLECTIVE TASK

Think about the different people you are or may be working with. How do they contribute to ensure the needs of the learners are met?

The members of the team you may have identified are:

- your mentor;
- other teachers/lecturers;
- your learners' mentor;
- programme/course leader;
- curriculum/section manager;
- learning support worker;
- basic skills tutor;

- subject learning coach/teaching and learning coach;
- advanced practitioner;
- exams officer;
- librarian;
- admissions officer;
- head of department.

Remember

In your organisation, the roles and responsibilities of staff members may be located under different titles. Together with their roles and responsibilities let's look at the college structure of the Skills for Life (SfL) department at a local college of further education.

Principal of the college

The principal has overall responsibility for the running of the college at a strategic level. This means being concerned with the overall direction of the entire institution.

Assistant principal of teaching and learning

This role includes responsibility for the standard of teaching and learning across the college. This person is proactively involved in ensuring that the college strives for excellence and works at a strategic level.

Curriculum manager SfL provision

A strategic level post, this position requires managing the SfL section and ensuring its smooth running.

Curriculum leader for SfL (subject coach)

This is a management post at operational level. This person may complete timetables for the team and liaise with examination bodies regarding the accreditation offered to the learners. This role provides a bridge between senior management and those working in the class-room. A curriculum leader may also take on the role of a subject coach. This will offer them the opportunity to share best practice and develop staff training for the team.

Senior lecturer (mentor)

This is likely to be a teacher with a few years' teaching experience who may be allocated the role of mentor. Together with being a mentor to trainee teachers the senior lecturer may also be a mentor to new staff.

Lecturer

The person in this role is often a recently qualified teacher. This is the role those in-service may be undertaking or those in pre-service will be applying for on completion of the programme. As a lecturer, you will have your own classes and be responsible for delivering effective lessons and for accurate record keeping.

PRACTICAL TASK PRACTICAL TASK **PRACTICAL TASK** PRACTICAL TASK **PRACTICAL TASK**

Research

Find out the structure of the organisation you work in or are on placement in. This is not only useful in gaining an understanding of how the organisation structure operates but also offers you the opportunity to look at how your career can progress.

Communication

In working to meet the needs of your learners it will be essential that you communicate effectively and work well within your team, across the college and where appropriate within a multidisciplinary partnership.

Many of you will bring with you current and innovative skills which you can share with other trainees and qualified tutors. For example, if you are teaching hairdressing you may be fresh from working in a salon and be up to date with the latest techniques. Sharing your knowledge and skills can be very rewarding.

However, for others it may also be frustrating if it is felt the skills are not being utilised. For example, if you have been a manager in your previous employment and held a great deal of responsibility and status, not having the same autonomy as a trainee teacher can prove to be a difficult learning curve. You may encounter incidents you once had the power to change but cannot now because you are the most junior member of the team. Remember you are building another career and need to develop your knowledge in this new area. The skills you have are transferable; the opportunity to use them will come at different stages in your new career. PCET providers can be truly inspiring places to work in. This is enhanced if the team you work alongside has a congenial atmosphere in which colleagues are supportive and work well together. I still recall how, surrounded by a really positive team, I thrived in my first teaching job. Passionate about the learners, we shared ideas over our coffee breaks and there was always plenty of dialogue on how we could move forward and develop further innovative approaches to our teaching. This often led to sharing resources and team teaching.

What was effectively built was what Lave and Wenger (1991) described as *situational learning* whereby I worked in close contact with experienced members of the team and others in their *communities of practice* (1991, pp97–91).

However, in some busy departments, office politics can exist and working within teams can prove difficult. For a trainee teacher or new teacher this can be draining. A point to remember is that you are on a journey and in order for it to be rewarding and productive it is important to recognise that *in a profession where time is precious and where the demands of the workplace are considerable, does it not make sense to work together where possible and desirable, in order to make the working day that little less stressful and more enjoyable?* (Tummons, 2007, p56). A way to do this is to stay out of the office politics and keep focused on what your aim is – to be a successful teacher in the LLS.

CASE STUDY
Kevin – training to teach law

Researching my placement organisation in advance was important to me for two main reasons. Firstly, quite naturally, I wanted to know what kind of organisation I would be going into. Our professional placement was to be scheduled over a period of 18 weeks and was therefore a major part of the course. Consequently I needed to know about the environment in which I would be undertaking my 'teaching practice'.

The second reason for researching the organisation in advance was that before the organisation would accept me on placement, they wanted to interview me. An interview was therefore arranged with the person at the college who was responsible for the department in which I was going to be placed and I was conscious that, if I was going to be interviewed, I needed to be able to have a knowledgeable discussion with the interviewer which demonstrated the fact that I was keen to participate effectively in the life of the college and the department where I was to be placed. In addition, I thought having knowledge of the way the college operated would allow me to ask important questions about the teaching I would be doing.

I therefore set about researching before this initial interview with the college and my first port of call was the college website. The college is a major provider of further education and, I think, the largest further education college in the country. The website provided an overview of the college itself and its history. I was also interested in the ethos of the college and looked at its 'Strategic Vision', which mentioned provision of excellence in learning and training, recruitment of learners from the widest range of groups locally, nationally and internationally and provision of a high-quality, flexible service for employers. This gave me an indication that the college would provide opportunities for both local and overseas students and that some course provision would be designed with the needs of the local community and employers in mind.

I next looked at website description of the range of courses provided and narrowed down my search to include only those programmes which involved my specialist subject area, law. I found that in this subject area the college offered A level law (AS and A2) at a number of its sites. However, this was not taught at the site where I was to undertake my placement. Instead, at that site, the college offered courses leading to awards made by the Institute of Legal Executives (ILEX) at level 3 and level 6 of the National Qualifications Framework.

These are courses which can lead to qualification as a Fellow of the Institute of Legal Executives (the third branch of the legal profession, with barristers and solicitors being the other two) or can provide an alternative route to qualification as a solicitor. As such, these courses were taught in the Professional Programmes department of the college. In addition, this department provided higher education courses in business and accountancy, some of which had a law component. I therefore had a starting point for research on what I would actually be teaching and next visited the ILEX website to find that the college provided courses in a large range of substantive and practice law subjects, such as criminal law, civil litigation, family law, European law, land law and contract law.

Armed with this knowledge I was able to attend the interview at the college with the divisional leader for Professional Programmes and was confident that I could have a fruitful discussion with her. The 'interview' turned out really to be a very informal chat in which we covered my experience of teaching and of legal practice. We were joined by a couple of members of the law teaching team and there was discussion on which subjects, out of the wide range of those offered, I felt I had a sufficiently comprehensive subject knowledge to allow me to teach.

I felt it important to indicate to the team that I was flexible and would try my best to accommodate the team in covering the subjects which they were keen to have covered within the limits of my abilities. However, the process was very much one of constructive negotiation and I must say that immediately I felt that my experience and opinion were valued. The staff I met seemed really pleased to be welcoming me as a member of the team. This was obviously very reassuring. Within a couple of days of the interview a timetable had been arranged by email correspondence and a date was arranged when I would start the shadowing and observing phase of my placement.

In the meantime, I continued my research, looking at and printing off all the relevant information with regard to the curriculum offered by the college and, in particular, the subjects which I would be teaching. For my own satisfaction, I needed to have a 'road map' of where I was going and what I was covering with each subject. This involved acquiring a detailed knowledge of the specifications for each subject.

It had been decided that, in the first semester, I would teach civil litigation, contract law and legal research and I was really pleased and reassured to see that I was quite comfortable with my knowledge of each of the topics to be covered in each of the subjects. However, I knew that I would have to do some reading to make sure that my subject knowledge was current, particularly in civil litigation where the rules change frequently.

Remember

Depending on your setting and whether you are pre-service or in-service, the information you need will vary. However, key information you need to be aware of is detailed in the check list below.

Check list

Health and safety Information.

- Do they have a health and safety policy?
- Who is the health and safety representative?
- Who is the first-aider in the department?
- If there is an accident what is the procedure?
- Look on the website for health and safety details.

Relevant policies that impact on your role, e.g. Every Child Matters, Equality and Diversity, Safeguarding, etc.

- Can you access these via the intranet?
- Is there a department quality portfolio containing key policies?

The curriculum area you are teaching.

- What level students will you be teaching? e.g. GCSE English or basic skills or both.
- What is the age range of your learners?

- What facilities do the classrooms have you will be teaching in? e.g. do you have a smartboard and projector to use PowerPoint?
- Do you have access to the learners' screening and diagnostic results? These are an important starting point to build a personalised curriculum which meets the specific needs of your learners.
- How many learners are in each class?
- What is the make-up of the cohort you are teaching in terms of gender and ethnicity?
- What are the learners' learning styles?
- What times are you delivering the lessons?

Where will you be located?

- Do you have a desk you can work at when you are not teaching?
- Do you have somewhere you can store your files?
- Are there facilities where you can go for your lunch?
- Can you access the college intranet to put students' work on line? You will need an account number; who provides that?
- Can you access a library card while you are there?
- Where are the nearest toilets?
- Where is the photocopying machine?
- Are there tea- and coffee-making facilities?
- Do you have access to the car park?

Factors to consider during your induction

The induction will offer you the opportunity to meet the staff you will be working alongside. For those of you in-service you may have already had an induction but may need to refresh your knowledge in the light of undertaking your teaching qualification. As a trainee teacher this is your opportunity to make an impression and importantly gain information about how the department operates. It may be your mentor who guides you through the induction process.

REFLECTIVE TASK

Make a list of the factors you will need to identify in your induction and note why they are important.

CASE STUDY
Kevin outlines his induction

My induction into college life was carried out on an informal basis and it appeared to me that induction is one of those things where you 'get out what you put in'. Therefore, the more you show a desire or willingness to be involved in college life apart from teaching, the more you learn about the college, its people and its systems. I asked for access to the college ICT network and an email account and was provided with these.

Unfortunately, the staff room was small and the desk I was allocated did not have a PC, but I was told that I could use the desk and PC of any member of staff who was not in college at that time. I was therefore careful to make sure that I knew when other teachers were not going to be present before I used their desks. I know that I would find it irritating if I turned up to find someone else using my desk.

Having access to the network was invaluable as I could be included in team emails and could access the college's intranet to look at notices and announcements. The other thing which was invaluable was the code for the photocopier.

In addition, while on induction, I made sure that I asked questions about the small, but (I thought) important things such as the names and locations of people who could solve problems. These included the ITC support staff who could be called upon if the IT facilities did not work in the classrooms, the admin person responsible for room bookings if there was a double booking. I ascertained the system for requesting mass photocopying of handouts and other resources, what the procedure was in the event of a fire alarm, and the procedures for completing class registers.

I think that it's definitely the case that the more you show an interest in people and the organisation, the more colleagues will be interested in your welfare and progress and the more they will want to include you as a full member of the team. One very experienced member of staff said to me at the start of my placement, *If you want to get a job here at the end of your training, the best thing to do is to make yourself indispensable while you are on placement!*

Understanding and organising your teaching file

Your teaching file is an essential part of your teaching experience. As such you should ensure your file/portfolio is kept organised and up to date. The contents and structure of a teaching file will vary across teaching providers and each organisation.

PRACTICAL TASK PRACTICAL TASK PRACTICAL TASK PRACTICAL TASK PRACTICAL TASK

List what you think should be in a teaching file.

CASE STUDY
What Sally (specialism – Travel and Tourism) included in her teaching file and why
Initial audit: This was completed at the beginning of the course so I could identify any gaps in my skills and address them. For example, I could not use the smartboard, so an aim was to develop my ICT skills.

Teaching timetable: This kept a track of all the hours I had taught, together with the level and subject area. This was particularly relevant when I wanted to highlight the breadth of the teaching I had carried out. For example, I taught A level geography to a group of mature learners on a Monday morning, and in the afternoon I taught travel and tourism at BTEC First level to a cohort of 16-year-olds. Although very different, each of the classes pulled on my specialism of travel and tourism.

Proof of registration to professional bodies: Institute for Learning.

Observation paperwork: Eight successful tutor and mentor observation feedback forms. I also included my lesson plan, rationales, cohort analysis and all resources in this. The feedback from the observation fed into a revised action plan that was updated throughout the teaching practice.

Observation of experienced teachers. Although I observed colleagues teaching more than twice, on two occasions I recorded them. This allowed me the opportunity to really focus on the best practice I witnessed. I noted this down and tried to build it into my lessons.

For example, one tutor used PowerPoint really effectively. Whereas I had been initially putting a great deal of text on each slide, I noticed that this tutor just highlighted the main points. This allowed the lesson the flow well and the feedback from the students was good. The impact of this was that I reduced the text on my slides, facilitating more interaction with the students rather than me just reading out all the information.

LLUK standards: Tracking my achievement of the LLUK standards allowed me to tick off the ones I had successfully achieved so I knew any gaps I needed to address.

Reflections on my practice including critical incidents: It was very helpful to write my reflections. I tended to write them at the end of the day or if possible directly after the incident. I kept a small notebook in my bag that was easily accessible – I had filled three of them by the end of my teaching practice.

It was helpful to put together an action plan after the reflection, particularly when I wanted to address incidents that hadn't gone as well as I had planned. For example, I had a group of 16-year-olds that found it very hard to settle. I taught them on a Friday afternoon and they were very giddy. [For strategies on managing behaviour read Chapter 6.] Recording the impact of the changes I made was particularly rewarding as I could see real progress both in my practice and in the learners' behaviour.

A record of the mentor meetings: These will allow you to discuss any issues that have cropped up in your practice with your mentor. Building in time for mentor meetings is vital. (The role of the mentor is explored further in Chapter 5.)

Minimum core in literacy, numeracy and ICT: At the beginning of the programme I undertook an initial screening and diagnostic assessment in literacy, numeracy and ICT. This identified any gaps in my skills. Achieving the minimum core was tracked through assignments, placement, tutorials and importantly the interim and summative triangulation.

The minimum core is divided into two sections:

- knowledge and understanding;
- personal skills.

The minimum core was essential to my preparation in two ways.

1. To support me in developing inclusive approaches to learners with language, literacy and numeracy needs. There is a clear expectation that teachers will support students in developing their functional skills in literacy, numeracy and ICT, especially in relation to their specialist subject. This may be through embedding and contextualising functional/key skills into the specialist area. You may also need to work with other professionals who are specialists in teaching these areas.

2. To support me in identifying my own needs for literacy, numeracy and ICT skills, and to support and monitor the development of these skills through the tutoring and mentoring processes. Prior to the course I did not have a GCSE in mathematics. However, after working with a specialist tutor at the university I achieved my level two in numeracy. This was a real achievement. The certificate was kept in my portfolio, together with all other evidence in order to complete my action plan.

Remember

It is vital that an initial assessment of your personal skills in literacy, numeracy and ICT is carried out. An individual development plan should then be developed to include the development of these skills and any associated needs identified. This is in accordance with guidelines issued by LLUK. Full details of the minimum core and guidance and its inclusion in teaching qualifications is detailed in an LLUK document titled: *Addressing Literacy, Language, Numeracy and ICT needs in education and training: Defining the minimum core of teachers' knowledge, understanding and personal skills – A guide for initial teacher education programmes. (LLUK, 2007)*

CASE STUDY
Angela (specialism – psychology) describes how she organised her file
A couple of weeks before the first portfolio's hand-in deadline, I worked with another student on getting it right. For a week, we worked painstakingly through each section, calling out what should be in that section and identifying what was missing. We'd then go home, work on our respective missing bits, and meet up again the next day. The most time-consuming sections, by far, were recording the achievement of LLUK standards and minimum core, cross-referencing with work we'd done and feedback from tutors and mentors. I realised, during this period, that if I didn't start the second semester portfolio early and add to it every week or so, it had the potential to become another huge task, so I worked on it every few days. It was a far simpler job to do it that way. Much of it comprised gathering up everything from observed sessions and placing them in the correct sections, so it was about being organised and staying on top of things. It helped that I have an office at home with plenty of space.

Remember

A key member of your team is the mentor. As the subject specialist this is the person who will guide you throughout your professional placement. The mentoring you receive will be around practical teaching issues, systems, procedures and sometimes the personal problems you encounter, e.g. child care issues. However, importantly, meetings with your mentor should also allow you to engage in critical and reflective dialogue about your developing practice. This dialogue should be the key to reflection and development.

CASE STUDY
Angela's experience of initial teaching practice
I hit the ground running during my placement. Behind the scenes, my CRB check had been completed – the college insist on doing an additional one, even though the university does a CRB check on all PGCE students as a matter of course. There is a strong focus on safeguarding the learners, which is understandable. My mentor talked me through cohort analyses of the classes I'd be teaching, went through everything from the classroom disciplinary procedures to dealing with learners' various medical issues, and outlined health and safety procedures. I was shown around and introduced to the department's staff members, many of whom were former nurses, which was most reassuring when I discovered that one of my learners was heavily pregnant.

By the next day, I had a log-in account to the staff computer network and my own key to the classrooms I'd be using. I spent the next few days picking the brains of my mentor and her colleagues, making copious additional notes. Everyone was so generous with their time, even though I knew most people were extremely busy.

Taking account of key legislation and initiatives

As a trainee teacher you should register with the Institute for Learning (IfL). This is a professional body for teachers, trainers, tutors and student teachers in the further education (FE) sector. Its aim is to support the needs of its members and, importantly, raise the status of teaching practitioners across the sector.

The IfL, as the body responsible for the regulation of teachers' professional formation, has a role that is circumscribed in relation to a set of standards which need to be evidenced in order to achieve a licence to practice (IfL 2008). As with any area of work, tutors must work within the boundaries of the law and professional values. There is a large number of laws and professional ethics which are constantly changing or being updated. Your organisation will have its own policies and procedures relating to these legal requirements.

The Institute for Learning states:

> *The Institute for Learning values and promotes the autonomy of learning practitioners whilst aiding their individual and collective development within a framework of integrity, honesty and professionalism.*

> (IfL Handbook, 2008)

In this capacity it has six core principles:

- Integrity
- Care
- Disclosure

- Respect
- Practice
- Responsibility

As a practitioner it is vital that you are aware of the key legislation and policy in the Lifelong Learning Sector (LLS). (This will be fully explored in Chapter 7.) However, the task now is to research the organisational approach to equality and diversity at your placement. To support this you will need to identify key legislation.

The rationale behind this is rooted in recognising that your learners are individuals who should be treated as equals and with respect, irrespective of gender, marital status, sexual orientation, disability, race, nationality, ethnic origin, age, religion or belief, domestic circumstances, social or employment status. This means that you should not label learners or have favourites. You should also ensure that your classroom is one based on respect for yourself and the learners.

PRACTICAL TASK PRACTICAL TASK **PRACTICAL TASK** PRACTICAL TASK **PRACTICAL TASK**

Identify the key documents in relation to equal opportunities and your teaching role in PCET.

Some of the key documents relating to equal opportunities are:

- Equal Pay Act (1970)
- Rehabilitation of Offenders Act (1974)
- Sex Discrimination Act (1975)
- Race Relations Act (1976, 2000)
- Disability Discrimination Act (1995 and subsequent regulations)
- Human Rights Act (1998)
- Employment Equality (Sexual Orientation) Regulations (2003)
- Employment Equality (Religion or Belief) Regulations (2003)
- Employment Equality (Age) Regulations (2006)
- Gender Equality Duty 2007

Policy

There are a number of key policies you will need to be aware of; these will be covered in detail in Chapter 7. A key policy that will impact on how you shape your teaching practice is Every Child/Learner Matters (EC/LM).

Tutors within the LLS sector need to be accountable for their contribution to improving the outcomes for children and young people. In this capacity it is essential that they display a responsive and meaningful attitude to their learners' well-being. 'Personalisation' is a term that is used to refer to the complete learner experience for each individual, to attain the objectives of Every Child Matters (ECM). Personalisation strategies must be applied to every step of learning and the student's development. This will include developing holistic programmes which move away from a deficit model of curriculum design (Duckworth, 2008).

Within this context the ability to meet the needs of all students is essential. Part of this ability means recognising and addressing your learners in terms of their culture and what it is that motivates them. You also need to be aware of why students might lack motivation; have they continually faced failure; what are the barriers to learning they face?

ECM requires teachers to collaborate with others who have a contribution to make to the educational progress and well-being of the learners. A driving feature of this is a multi-agency approach to assist students in navigating their way through the educational system and in finding opportunities for learning that are attuned to their personal needs and aspirations.

The five outcomes of Every Child Matters (ECM) are:

1. Being healthy
2. Staying safe
3. Enjoying and achieving
4. Making a positive contribution
5. Achieving economic well-being

REFLECTIVE TASK

How can you embrace the ECM outcomes into your practice?

You may have considered the following.

Information, advice and guidance.	• Access to good, meaningful careers. Progression routes, e.g. HE, link to support such as counsellors.
Preparation for working life.	• Opportunities for work-based learning for young people; apprenticeships. • Opportunities for enterprise and creative education. • Pre-foundation students learning independent living skills – e.g. learning to shop/budget, etc. • Offering a social practice model based on the context of the learners' lives (See Barton and Hamilton, 1998).
Development of skills needed for economic well-being.	• Development of a range of meaningful skills to ensure effective studying or working life, e.g. financial literacy, wider functional skills, punctuality, team-working opportunities, confidence building.

Examples of best practice

- Preparation for budgeting in Entry to Employment programme and Pre-Foundation programme.
- Financial literacy embedded into all programmes.
- Taster days at HE providers and HE days.
- Foundation students run a college shop selling their cakes, old books, bric-à-brac, etc.
- Young enterprise activity. Awards for innovative ideas. Links with business.

Record keeping

Accurate record keeping is an essential part of your day-to-day practice. As such you will encounter a variety of paperwork. Tackling it effectively will be essential in your role as a professional in the Lifelong Learning Sector.

PRACTICAL TASK PRACTICAL TASK **PRACTICAL TASK** PRACTICAL TASK **PRACTICAL TASK**

Find out what records you need to keep as a teacher.

You may have identified:

- registers;
- mark sheets;
- individual learning plans;
- disciplinary records;
- student support documentation.

Accountability is a vital component relating to your professional integrity. As such, keeping accurate records is essential. Failure to do so is classed as gross misconduct in many organisations.

Finally...

As a busy professional, using the **'SEE'** technique can promote an organised and productive approach to your working day. This means working:

S – Smartly
E – Effectively
E – Ending each day with your desk tidy.

You'll arrive to work each day with a clear deck ready for whatever challenges the new day brings!

A SUMMARY OF **KEY POINTS**

In this chapter we have:

> considered the structure of your organisation;

> explored the roles and responsibilities of all the key players;

> discussed the factors to consider during your induction;

> emphasised the understanding and organisation of your teaching file;

> discussed taking account of key legislation and initiatives, e.g. ECM.

REFERENCES REFERENCES REFERENCES REFERENCES REFERENCES REFERENCES

Appleby, Y (2004) *Literacy Today*, Issue no. 38.

Barton, D and Hamilton, M (1998) *Local Literacies: Reading and Writing in One Community*. Abingdon: Routledge.

Barton, D, Ivanic, R, Appleby, Y, Hodge, R and Tusting, K (2007) *Literacy, Lives and Learning*. Abingdon, Routledge.

Duckworth, V (2008) *Getting Better Worksheets*. Gate House Books.

Gravells, A and Simpson, S (2008) *Planning and Enabling Learning in the Lifelong Learning Sector*. Exeter: Learning Matters.

Lave, J and Wenger, E (1991) *Situated Learning. Legitimate Peripheral Participating*. Cambridge. Cambridge University Press.

LLUK (2007) *Addressing Literacy, Language, Numeracy and ICT Needs in Education and Training: Defining the minimum core of teachers' knowledge, understanding and personal skills. A guide for initial teacher education programmes*. London: LLUK.

Tummons, T (2007) *Becoming a Professional Tutor in the Lifelong Learning Sector*. Exeter: Learning Matters.

Wenger, E (1998) *Communities of Practice: Learning, Meaning and Identity*. Cambridge: Cambridge University Press.

FURTHER READING FURTHER READING FURTHER READING FURTHER READING

Duckworth, V (2009) *'Into Work' 14–19 series*. Gate House Books.

Gravells, A and Simpson, S (2008) *Planning and Enabling Learning in the Lifelong Learning Sector*. Exeter: Learning Matters.

Petty, G (2004) *Teaching Today*. Nelson Thornes.

> This is an excellent book that covers the basics of teaching in the Post-Compulsory sector in an enjoyable and readable way.

Reece, I and Walker, S (2006) *Teaching Training and Learning*. Business Education Publishers Ltd.

> This book covers the whole range of issues you may encounter in your practice. It also offers useful techniques to develop your teaching and learning strategies. It is a great read for new teachers.

Tummons, J (2007) *Assessing Learning in the Lifelong Learning Sector*. Exeter: Learning Matters.

Websites

Department for Business Innovation and Skills (formerly DCSF)

> **www.dcsf.gov.uk**

Institute for Learning

> **www.ifl.ac.uk**

Lifelong Learning UK

> **www.lluk.org**

Standards Verification UK

> **www.standardsverificationuk.org**

2
Planning your sessions

The objectives of this chapter

The purpose of this chapter is to provide a context for two key elements of your observed teaching practice: the scheme of work and the session plan. By drawing on practical experience I hope to provide the motivation to consider both of these planning tools as fundamental cornerstones of your success.

By the end of this chapter you should be able to recognise the difference between course-level programming using a scheme of work and session-level planning using a session plan. Each of these planning tools offers different support for your teaching and you will be able develop both.

Please note throughout this chapter the term 'lesson' is taken to mean a learning event whether it takes places in a classroom, workshop, laboratory or lecture theatre and is interchangeable with 'session' – see LLUK Standard DK1.2 below.

It addresses the following professional practice standards for QTLS:

AK 4.1 Principles, frameworks and theories which underpin good practice in learning and teaching.

BK 2.1 Principles of learning and ways to provide learning activities to meet curriculum requirements and the needs of all learners.

BK 3.3 Ways to structure and present information and ideas clearly and effectively to learners.

DK 1.1 How to plan appropriate, effective, coherent and inclusive learning programmes that promote equality and engage with diversity.

DK 1.2 How to plan a teaching session.

DK 2.1 The importance of including learners in the planning process.

Introduction

Planning is bringing the future into the present so that you can do something about it now.

Alan Lakein

PRACTICAL TASK PRACTICAL TASK **PRACTICAL TASK** PRACTICAL TASK **PRACTICAL TASK**

1. Write down, now, the date of the final class for the course(s) you are teaching.
2. If you teach on a course with external examinations, write down, now, the date of the examination(s).
3. If you teach on a course with assessed coursework such as portfolios or assignments, write down, now, the final date for submission.

Reflection

How successful were you in doing this?

If you don't know the answers, you need to find out quickly.

Try this next activity.

PRACTICAL TASK PRACTICAL TASK PRACTICAL TASK PRACTICAL TASK PRACTICAL TASK

1. How many weeks does your course last for?
2. How many sessions will you deliver during that time?
3. When are the holidays in the year: half-term, Christmas, Easter?
4. When does your organisation close to take these holidays?
5. Are there any festivals from other local faith communities that need to be included when identifying total time available to teach?

The first stage of your planning needs to consider and address the overall timescale and then to break the course up into component parts that are appropriate in terms of demand, duration, coherence and assessment. This is the function of the scheme of work.

Planning courses – the scheme of work

A scheme of work may be known by other names – course programme, course scheme, curriculum overview, course overview – but 'scheme of work' has been a constant term during my 27 years in the sector and it will serve its purpose. The essence of a scheme of work is that it is the starting point of your planning.

Many trainees find it difficult to see the difference between a scheme of work and a session plan given that they appear to address the same issues, namely planning and delivery of a session. However, it is the scale and purpose of each that makes them different and valuable in their own way. The scheme of work takes the bigger picture, the course as a whole with attention to the level and to the learners, to its start and end, and to the structure and delivery of content and the assessment strategies that need to be addressed.

There is an oft-repeated dictum: to fail to plan is to plan to fail. Failure in terms of overall course planning would result in running out of time to cover all the course content; not building in time for draft submissions of assignments or revision before examinations; not having work ready for external moderation or verification; contributing to the anxiety of learners by making their learning feel unnecessarily rushed; not allocating appropriate time to reflect different demands in course content; and so on.

All these are avoidable and a properly prepared and continually used scheme of work will address these risks.

Developing the scheme of work – confirming actual teaching responsibilities

Starting with the basics, there is nothing more fundamental then finding out what you are going to be teaching. This applies equally to pre-service and in-service staff. You will need to speak to other members of your team if you are an in-service trainee or to your mentor if you are a pre-service trainee. Either way, you need to know as soon as possible your timetable and the course(s), their levels and the actual groups for which you will be responsible.

You must be proactive. You may have a wonderful mentor or colleagues who will anticipate your every need and go out of their way to meet them. On the other hand, the sector is generally agreed to be overworked and understaffed, so you might just have to get on with it.

While you should accept any information about your course and your timetable courteously and gratefully, do not expect it to do everything for you in terms of planning. How one person conceives of a course and its sessions does not mean that it will match your style of teaching or the style of this current group of learners. Nor will it necessarily be best practice: it is no excuse to say *but this is what I was given*.

We expect our trainees to be critically evaluative and even where a scheme and plans are set you are asked to take the opportunity for reflection and critical evaluation.

Developing the scheme of work format

A sample document is shown in Appendix 1 on page 121.

There will be other formats and you should scrutinise any that you come across to ensure you can make the best possible use of them. There will sometimes be a noticeable variation between document formats provided by a training institution and the place where teaching practice is being undertaken.

You may be offered a poor design of scheme of work but be required by your mentor to complete this in order to maintain consistency within the section or department. It may be that your tutor can develop a conversation with the mentor about the relative merits of the different documents but at this point it is better to go along with the requirements of your host college.

While it is to be hoped that common sense would prevail and that no trainee would be put in the position of having to complete two types of paperwork for one purpose, you should take the opportunity to reflect on and comment on the difference in format and show how the use of one over the other might facilitate your planning of teaching and subsequently the quality of learning.

You may be offered a completed scheme of work. While this is a useful starting point it may be necessary to exercise some critical reflection (see Chapter 4) in order to demonstrate secure coverage for the LLUK standards pertinent to planning of teaching and learning.

For the full teacher role, QTLS, as described by LLUK, you do need to be able to produce your own scheme of work and not just rely on existing examples. The LLUK Standard DK1.2

(see above) expects knowledge of how to plan but you are also actually required to plan and to produce your own documents. (See LLUK DP1, DP1.2 and DP1.3).

A good scheme has number of elements that are fundamental to secure planning, including:

- course;
- learner cohort;
- duration and structure;
- sequence and weighting;
- session outcomes and assessment.

Course

Check and double-check the course(s) you are being asked to teach. Is there a copy of the current course specification? Not last year's but this year's; not the one 'we've always taught' but the one you should be teaching.

You can check on individual awarding body websites or, for a one-stop solution, the National Database of Qualifications (NDAQ) on the Qualifications and Curriculum Development Agency (QCDA) website.

Information about the assessment requirements and associated deadlines can be found in these documents and committed to your scheme of work (as well as to your diary and your memory). Awarding bodies have hundreds of thousands of pieces of candidates' work to deal with and cannot manage late submissions within the very tight deadlines they have.

REFLECTIVE TASK

Consider how you would explain to your learners/their parents/your principal why they received such poor marks in their A level coursework because you failed to know the full requirements.

The position on coursework continues to change across qualifications and subjects following the QCA Report, *A review of GCE and GCSE coursework arrangements*, published in November 2005, and you should check carefully the arrangements for your particular subject.

Learner cohort

As you can see from our template in Appendix 1, the front of the scheme of work has a section for collecting some basic information about your learners. You may wish to add extra boxes to capture details you consider pertinent. You may find some redundant, but we would certainly advocate seeking to make effective use of this sort of planning.

Learners are people: they have hopes and needs, confidence and concerns, motivations and barriers. A professional and fully engaged teacher is aware of this and allows these factors to inform planning where possible and where relevant.

This is not a proposition that courses can be fine-tuned to the extent that every individual need can be met on every occasion: that's usually not possible. However, going to the trouble of finding out the sort of information suggested will be a valuable exercise on several levels.

You may have to go and speak to other tutors and non-teaching staff to find out some of the necessary information. In this way you begin to develop the valuable network that will assist you both as a pre-service or in-service trainee. You will find out the role and responsibilities of those involved in registration and examinations, of those involved in induction, initial assessment and learning support.

In undertaking these activities you will come to know your learners better and this will communicate itself to them. They may feel more valued because you are clearly getting to know them and their needs and this, in turn, may be reflected in better motivation on their part.

Duration, weighting and sequence

Think of the basics. What have I got to cover, how much time have I got and what is the best sequence and duration of topics? Where are the exams (GCSE, A level or similar) and where are the internal moderation/verification deadlines and the external deadlines?

What is the calendar like this year? You may think that an odd question but in 2008, Easter was earlier than it had been for nearly 100 years, falling on 23 March, the last time that had happened being 1913. In 2011 Easter will be 24 April, the next to latest day it can be, something that is happening only twice in the twenty-first century. (2095 is the next year, since you ask, but I doubt if you'll have to worry about that!).

What these changes do is to create significant swings in the length of the spring and summer terms. An early Easter can create terms of only eight weeks (depending on what your organisation does about half-terms), while a late Easter can provide a 12-week term but then a rush between the holiday break and the start of revision, exams and portfolio building. Furthermore, depending on the local context there may be implications to the timetable where there are feasts in the calendar of learners from different cultures.

You also need to consider whether all topics in the specification, and thus in your scheme of work, need an equal amount of time. They probably don't but you must look at the assessment strategy used – number of exams, weightings of marks, mandatory topics and so on – in determining how much time to invest in any topic.

CASE STUDY
A level biology in a grammar school on Merseyside
From my own experience, many years ago, we were poorly served by a teacher of A level biology who in the first year covered only about one-tenth of the syllabus because he was too enthusiastic and too knowledgeable about the first topic to move past it.

His replacement (the school had spotted the problem) had to take us through the remaining content at such a pace that comprehensive knowledge and understanding were always going to be difficult to achieve.

The examination was weighted equally across all parts of the syllabus (as it was called then) to the disadvantage of all learners.

Of course, confronted with a list of modules or units, with aims and outcomes, it is not obviously clear how the course should be divided up. The important advice here – to borrow from the popular IT idiom – is 'RTM!' (read the manual).

Too many people give a skim-read to the most valuable document provided by award-bodies, namely the specification (sometimes called the syllabus or standards depending on the age and type of qualification). The names vary but the premise is the same: this is what we want you to teach and this is how it will be assessed.

CASE STUDY
Teaching AEB A level psychology in 1988

When I taught A level psychology the syllabus said early on, in clear, large letters, that there would be so many questions on each of the syllabus areas; that there would be another question about the broad approach of psychology; that there would be six pieces of coursework required and they had to be in the following types and so on.

This was information enough to make a realistic analysis of the content to be covered and the time that each topic was broadly going to take. However, it was not simply a numerical strategy. Because of subject expertise a teacher may know well that some content is more challenging, more difficult to grasp; or that, despite the apparent details provided in the specification, this particular topic may look substantial but is fairly compact and accessible. However, creating a different challenge, the syllabus required the teaching of biological approaches to psychology, something my own degree had not included. At the time it was difficult to find advice and it would be dishonest not to admit to being 'one chapter ahead of the students' for the first time I taught it.

Nowadays awarding bodies signpost changes to specification content very clearly, often running teacher workshops led by subject experts to ensure effective dissemination of relevant information. Sites such as Teachernet provide many valuable resources with regard to planning.

And, of course, the use of search engines will return copious material on subject content. Use discerningly.

In addressing the order in which you wish to teach, assuming there are no directed prerequisites from the awarding body, a sensible strategy is to start with a topic that you are confident with and that you know well so as to allow some time for the necessary reading to facilitate your command of the less familiar work.

Many subject groups have an annual conference that would look at specification, content and assessment strategies. As chief examiner for the Southern Examining Group's GCSE psychology I was expected to attend the Association of Teachers of Psychology annual conference for this purpose.

The remaining, obvious point is to ask your colleagues or your mentor for advice and, at this point in your career, to take it.

Session outcomes and assessment

One immediate benefit of a well-written and clearly presented scheme of work is the sense of course overview it provides. By quickly reading over five or six pages you will develop an appreciation of what you have done in terms of teaching, learning and assessment. If you see page after page of 'lecture', 'lecture', 'lecture', perhaps it is a reminder to think a little more about your learners, how they learn and the match between content and activity. If you are teaching a practical course and just have a list of 'workshop' with no more detail, then you are missing the opportunity to check coverage, variation, resourcing, assessment and so on.

Trainees often ask why they have to provide learning objectives or outcomes on a scheme of work and again on a session plan. Well, the reality is that in these days of omniscient technology you will only have to write them once. After that they can be cut and pasted into the individual plan. What it does do is to secure coverage of the course at both the macro and micro level.

By recording the assessment activity for each session on the scheme it serves as a reminder that this needs to be done but also allows you to plan strategically towards any formal assessment within the course. Any such formal assessments need to be emphasised and the dates and lead-in times shared regularly with our learners.

Planning sessions – the development of an effective session plan

The move from scheme of work to session plan is an act of drilling down to the detail. The session plan takes on the role of a script. Not in the sense of a word-by-word discourse but a clear road map of the session providing a running order of activities broken down into those of teacher and those of learner.

It will indicate the resources required at each point, a reminder that assessment of learning must be built into the session and will offer scope to signpost necessary details such as completing the register and recording progress in the session, directed work set and an evaluation for your own and your tutor's and mentor's consideration.

Developing the session plan format

A sample document is shown in Appendix 2 on page 123.

As with the scheme of work, session plan formats will vary from organisation to organisation and thus, in accord with the advice given previously, they may need to be compliant with what your employer or placement requires but this should be negotiated and evaluated.

CASE STUDY
Informal research into session plan formats used in post-compulsory education
Trainees were asked to submit examples of the session plans they were required to use at their placements.

Of the sample of 12 received there were no common layouts and little consistency of approach. There were variations in the use of the terms 'learning objective' and 'learning outcome'; variations in what the plan required in terms of teacher/learner

---

activity; variations in what was required for the recording of the assessment activity. Only three required aspects of Every Child Matters to be identified and/or recorded. Most used the term 'key skills'. One referred to 'essential skills', some just to categories of communication or numeracy.

Front page – general information

Make sure the information is accurate and consistent. If it is week 17 on the session plan, does it match week 17 on your scheme of work? It may not do so because of changes but so long as these have been annotated somewhere that is fine.

These are working documents – write on them, amend them, use them. They do not have to look pristine: in the event of an inspection it will be better that they look battered and worn out – at least they will show purpose.

Aims and objectives

There are variations on the use of learning objectives and learning outcomes, with many authors using them interchangeably. We have adopted the term 'learning objectives', drawing from Bloom's work and the behavioural objectives.

Aims are a general statement of intent – one or two per lesson is the recommendation, possibly three if you have a long workshop. Aims are best expressed from the teacher's point of view.

Objectives should follow from the aim(s), and if achieved will consolidate specific content from the course specification. One popular strategy is that objectives should be SMART (there are acceptable variations to each word in the mnemonic).

- **S**pecific: be clear, state in a straightforward way what learning will take place.
- **M**easurable: where appropriate, apply a standard to learner performance. Do you want learners to 'wire a plug' or 'wire a plug correctly'?
- **A**chievable: for the level of learners and with cognisance of resources available.
- **R**elevant: based on what the specification of the course requires.
- **T**imely: of a size and scope that is possible to be achieved within the duration of the session.

There is a useful formula which will help you write objectives: *by the end of this session, learners will be able to . . .* and then you insert your objective. For example:

- by the end of this session learners will be able to draw and describe a cross-section of an evergreen leaf;
- by the end of this session learners will be able to cook sauté potatoes correctly;
- by the end of this session learners will be able to provide an outline explanation of Newton's first law of motion.

Choose the language of your objectives carefully. Remember they are 'learning objectives' so must be appropriate to the session content.

For lessons dealing with knowledge and understanding use words like state, describe, explain, evaluate, summarise, compare, distinguish, analyse. For practical lessons it might be cut, apply, prepare, dress, drill, demonstrate.

Avoid words like 'understand' – often too broad; or phases like 'be familiar with', 'have a grasp of' – too vague; what do they actually mean? On occasion one sees objectives written as 'students will be aware of'. Is this SMART enough – I've sat in a classroom and heard the teacher talk about X. I'm now aware of it (the topic) but is that learning?

For every objective you do have – and three to five is often the optimum – you need an assessment strategy, a way of measuring each learner's achievement of each of these objectives.

Aims and objectives should be shared with learners at the start of the lesson but can be rephrased into more appropriate language depending on the learners and level of course. Objectives should be checked with the learners at the end of the lesson to demonstrate achievement.

Differentiation

With the increasing emphasis on personalised learning it is important that your session should show planned differentiation. This means that, as far as practicable, teaching strategies should aim to meet the differing needs and abilities of individual students. This implies the ability to challenge the more able while at the same time supporting those with lower abilities. This can be done and recorded within your objectives and also in the actual plan. Objectives can be differentiated with the formula of 'all learners will...', 'most learners will...', 'some learners will...'.

However, take care with this pattern if this does not reflect the specification accurately. Otherwise you may be planning a session in which you are intending some of your learners not to achieve what the awarding body expects.

Our target is always 'all learners' with regard to the basic core content of the session. 'Most' and 'some' must be tied into stated extension tasks reflected in the qualification assessment, such as grades or examination tiers. You can also provide differentiation by having a variety of activities and a variety of assessments against your objectives.

PRACTICAL TASK PRACTICAL TASK PRACTICAL TASK PRACTICAL TASK PRACTICAL TASK

1. Write three learning objectives for a topic you are to teach.
2. Now add one more in a differentiated style to extend any learners who successfully complete the core objectives within the lesson.

Notes

In our format you are provided with a useful working area.

Don't get lazy. The temptation is to cut and paste, just changing week numbers: don't do this. Here is the opportunity to check: has there been a room change? did you book the DVD player? what about the four students on the field trip? is the homework due in today? are you returning the draft assignments?

Functional skills and other areas of focus

As is noted in Chapter 7, the post-compulsory sector is ever-changing. Different institutions pursue different agendas and their paperwork often reflects this. If an Ofsted report has said a college doesn't focus enough on Every Child Matters, you can rest assured that the planning paperwork will change to address this. However, you must allow for some variation and variability so do not see these areas on your plan as beyond adaptation to local needs. These are your plans – discuss them with you mentor, tutor, colleagues, line manager to optimise their use.

Timing

This is an area that provokes a lot of dissatisfaction among trainees – *How am I meant to know how long something will take?*

This is where your cohort analysis comes in. How many are in the group? What does the activity involve?

If you have a round robin asking every learner for a one-word answer then 20 contributions may only take a minute or two. But if they are asked for a discussion response, even if this is only 30 seconds, it will take a least 10 minutes. If you have gone to break-out groups and they are feeding back, it could be five groups of four and they might each have three minutes' worth of input. You need to think about capturing contributions by writing them up, giving praise and feedback.

Clearly it is not possible to plan to the second but it *is* possible to chunk your session into likely periods. You should certainly have a reasonable estimate of any initial presentation – talk, video, demonstration, PowerPoint – because all of these are susceptible to timing issues.

But what if the learners are enthusiastic, if they interrupt with pertinent and keen observations and comments? What if it goes well and generates numerous questions moving the topic on? Here you have to decide if the input part of the session is amenable to these sorts of interruptions. I would generally insist the answer is yes. Don't flatten enthusiasm.

But you can manage it by indicating that you will take questions at set points, or at the end or whenever. You can factor in questions/discussion for, say, five minutes so that a 15-minute presentation becomes a 20-minute presentation plus Q&A. In the event of there being no significant Q&A you could have a quick quiz ready to add to the end of the session.

Again, looking at the format of session plans our small survey provided, it is noticeable that there is significant variety in the basic duration of a classroom session. This ranged across 35 to 120 minutes, with some organisations using 'single' and 'double' sessions while others had one standard length. You will need to plan according to local preferences.

Learner and teacher activity

A basic strategy for a session is to have some exposition, telling the learners what the session will be, then input of information and resources, followed by activity by the learners and assessment of progress within the session. If you only have 35 minutes you are going to have to be quick. If you have two hours you probably need to move through this cycle more than once to avoid loss of momentum.

Opinions differ as to the 'typical' concentration span for learners but it is commonly calculated as chronological age + 1 in minutes for teenagers, levelling off at about 20 minutes for adults. Coupling this with the requirement to address preferred learning styles, the need for a variety of activities becomes evident.

Assessment strategy

These activities need to be recorded for learner and teacher as appropriate. If you tie these activities to your learning objectives and across to your assessment strategy, you will have the basis for an effective session.

Assessment strategies do not mean full-blown assignments: question and answer, quizzes, quick tests, peer assessments, self-assessment are some of the basic tools. What is needed is a strategy that shows how each learner's achievement of the learning objectives has been measured and recorded.

There is an effective link to evaluation if you make good use of assessment strategies as you will be able to judge how effective the lesson was and how much learning took place. If you find yourself unable to make a judgement about that, then clearly you need to address assessment in your targets. If you know how the groups got on but not the individuals, then change the assessment activity for the next session to ensure every learner hands you something.

Evaluation

As mentioned above, this is a live document. A couple of points scribbled on at the end of the session may be more valuable, then neatly typing up a new version three days later. Your target setting can be transferred to the rationales required for assessed observations, to your reflective accounts in your personal development portfolio and will be an excellent starting point when meeting with your mentor or tutor.

A SUMMARY OF **KEY POINTS**

In this chapter we have:

> discussed breaking down your curriculum and designing schemes of work;

> emphasised the need to work within curriculum requirements;

> explored the issues involved in planning engaging sessions;

> considered the need to evaluate your planning and reflect on your development.

FURTHER READING FURTHER READING **FURTHER READING** FURTHER READING

Carr, D (2003) *Making Sense of Education*. RoutledgeFalmer.
    This book presents a more academic approach to understanding education and curriculum design and should enable you to extend your insight and develop critical understanding of the issues involved.
Jarvis, P, Holford, J and Griffin C (2003) *The Theory and Practice of Learning*. Abingdon: RoutledgeFalmer.
Tummons, J (2007) *Assessing Learning in the Lifelong Learning Sector*. Exeter: Learning Matters.
Tummons, J (2009) *Curriculum Studies in the Lifelong Learning Sector*. Learning Matters.
    This book considers the role of the curriculum and how to plan effective schemes of work. It is in a simple and easy-to-follow format.

Websites

National Qualifications Database
  www.accreditedqualifications.org.uk
Office of the Qualifications and Examinations Regulator
  www.ofqual.gov.uk
Qualifications and Curriculum Development Agency
  www.qcda.gov.uk

3
Your first observation

The objectives of this chapter

This chapter is designed to provide you with some guidance about your first observed teaching session, what to expect, what to prepare and what feedback you can expect. It is a very daunting experience being observed and it is important to be fully aware of your role in the process and that of your observer.

It addresses the following professional practice standards for QTLS:

BK 2.2 Ways to evaluate own practice in terms of efficiency and effectiveness.

DK 3.1 Ways to evaluate own role and performance in planning learning.

EK 4.2 The role of feedback in effective evaluation and improvement of own assessment skills.

Introduction

In times of change the learners will inherit the earth, while the knowers will find themselves beautifully equipped to deal with a world that no longer exists.

Eric Hoffer – Psychologist

As part of your training you will undertake a number of observed observations. According to LLUK there should be a minimum of eight observations, at least four of which should be carried out by a subject specialist. This means that your mentor will be involved in at least four observations and your tutor will carry out the others.

The observation process will vary depending on which organisation you are studying with; many organisations grade observations, but others do not. Again the documentation and procedures will vary. However, they will all be consistent in the extent to which they all meet the professional standards for teachers.

In this chapter we will consider the main components of the system but you will need to refer to your own procedures to ensure everything is covered when preparing for your observations. We will look at practical strategies for preparing yourself and at the rationale behind some of the processes involved.

The observation process

In order to encourage consistency of feedback and to provide clear evidence to support grading decisions/outcomes, standard documentation is used and in many organisations observations are graded using the Ofsted grading criteria shown below:

Grade 1 – Outstanding
Grade 2 – Good
Grade 3 – Satisfactory
Grade 4 – Unsatisfactory

All observations must be graded/deemed satisfactory or better to pass your training.

Guidance based on research and custom and practice states that the observer should be suitably qualified and experienced in conducting observations. They should have undertaken training in current observation procedures and should have carried out joint observations to ensure their competence to observe. Observers should sit somewhere that provides a good view of the trainee and the learner activities. This position may change but they should be unobtrusive at all times. They should be able to look at learners' work and speak to them if a suitable opportunity arises. The observer will observe a section of a lesson not normally longer than one hour and will formulate their grade/feedback based on evidence gathered at this time.

There are two types of observer: subject-specific mentors and observation tutors. Subject-specific mentors carry out four observations over the length of the programme and concentrate their observations on the accuracy of the trainee's subject knowledge and their ability to convey this to their learners.

Observation tutors will carry out four observations over the length of the programme and will focus on the planning and assessment of learning, the development of teaching and learning skills and strategies employed to ensure learning is taking place. Although they may comment on subject-specific issues if appropriate, these observers look at generic teaching and learning issues.

Throughout the eight observations the full range of the Lifelong Learning UK (LLUK) standards will be assessed and awarded if the trainee demonstrates competence in each one. This procedure is laid down by LLUK.

LLUK is the sector skills council (SSC) for lifelong learning. It supports all employers and employees in the Lifelong Learning Sector. The aim of LLUK is to develop a skilled workforce and nationally recognised set of standards and qualifications that are supported by employers, and which support the national skills targets. These standards define what is expected from teachers, trainers and tutors. They describe in generic terms the skills, knowledge and attitudes required of those who work in the sector (Lifelong Learning UK, 2008, p1).

Ofsted are concerned with ensuring that:

- trainees reach a satisfactory level of teaching competence against the main elements specified in the national qualification requirements;
- trainees have made sufficient progress in their teaching capability in relation to their prior attainment and experience (Ofsted, 2004, p4).

Observers are concerned with ensuring that these Ofsted criteria and the LLUK standards are met by trainees and that clear guidance is given to ensure competence is developed over the course of the programme.

The learning outcomes for the professional development modules of the programme require trainees to keep a portfolio of evidence of their teaching practice and as part of this they must include evidence of their observations and their reflections on their experience.

Some messages may be about improvements needed, about how to identify different ways of approaching less successful practice and/or how to reinforce and build on their best practice. Yet it is critical that the process of teacher observation is supportive and developmental. Therefore the observer will need to decide how to ensure the trainee feels valued throughout the process.

The ultimate purpose of the observation system is to help bring about improvements in the quality of the experience of your learners and their achievements. Observers cannot impose change, but can be catalysts in enabling individual trainees to identify possible changes and ways of bringing them about.

Targets for development should be owned by the trainee, be specific, measurable and achievable, have a direct impact on the experience of the learner and be monitored during the next observation.

The quality of teaching input is generally evaluated over a relatively long period, and takes into account the nature of the input, i.e. its appropriateness, its knowledge of learning theory, as well as one's skills as a lecturer and skills as a facilitator of learning.

Observation is an attempt to monitor and guarantee the quality of input into the placement organisation's teaching operations. Quality is all-important; it rarely emerges 'accidentally', but is a direct product of an effective teaching–learning partnership. Evaluation of staff should help to maintain the organisation's professional standards.

Most staff understand the necessity of honing their skills and keeping abreast of a rapidly changing educational environment and require feedback that enables them to understand their strengths and areas for development. This is especially important for trainee lecturers.

It is essential that the process adopted by the organisation fully embraces and ensures this quality of experience because trainees will want to know to what extent they are meeting the expectations of students and the organisation, and how they can develop their practice.

Observation is an important part in the continuous improvement of further education providers and in many colleges now any member of staff being given a grade 3 in an observation will be required to partake in extra training and then a re-observation.

The effect of this on teacher education is that it is no longer acceptable for teachers to qualify as 'satisfactory'. They need to achieve 'good' or 'outstanding' in their observations in order to gain employment in the sector. In order to support them in this aim we have to have systems that enable them to achieve this standard and allow them to maximise their potential. This includes observations that are consistent, fair and give them a real chance to get a high grade.

The structure of the 'reflective discussion' is very important and can make a huge difference to the observation process. *It is a question of feedback, really, of people getting the information essential to keep their efforts on track* (Goleman, 2005, p150). Although Goleman was discussing feedback in businesses and in marriages, this applies equally well to education. He identifies the need to be specific, offer a solution, be sensitive and to give the feedback face to face.

Within teacher education this 'reflective discussion' is often an area that is overlooked or paid lip service to. Feedback can often be formulaic and very general, leaving trainees with little to go on in order to improve in the future. Traditional approaches have included the 'feedback sandwich', giving praise, areas for improvement and then praise again. However, this technique is widely contested when giving verbal feedback.

> *To be honest, I have no idea why the sandwich feedback technique ever caught on, as the primacy and recency effect means it defeats its object. This effect describes what happens when we're given a long list of things to memorise. We remember most easily the first (primacy) and last (recency) things on the list and tend to forget the bits in the middle, which, in the case of feedback, is the very bit we want to be remembered.*

(Smart, 2003, p31)

When discussing feedback in relation to teacher observations it may be necessary for observers to choose carefully the content and the order of our feedback and to think about using clear targets for development to allow trainees to continue to develop their practice and to improve their teaching skills over time.

It is not necessary to describe the full content of a person or group participation in events, but rather to choose, judiciously, small details which are representative of action. Selected extracts are pithier and more appropriate for consideration, and provide illumination of possible usage while encouraging further reflection, dialogue and co-investigation.

Russell identifies 'Ten rules for giving feedback':

It should be balanced	*It should be specific*
It should be objective	*It should be appropriate*
It should be understandable	*It should be participative*
It should be comparable	*It should be actionable*
It should be sufficient	*It should be hierarchical*

(Russell, 1998, p156)

By 'hierarchical' he means that there is a limit to how much feedback a trainee teacher can absorb and this is often in the region of only three or four points. It is important to cover the most important point first, then the second most important point, and so on. If the threshold is reached by the fourth point, it is less of a problem. This conflicts slightly with Smart's theory, although both are agreed that the first thing we are told is memorable.

If you have any queries or concerns about the observation process or the feedback you receive, you should speak to your mentor or tutor and ask for clarification. It is imperative that you get the most out of the process in order to improve your practice in the future and to achieve your full potential.

CASE STUDY

Observation experience by Lorraine – training to teach psychology

I feel that I have developed enormously over the two years of teaching in many respects. The strengths that were highlighted in year one continue to be my greatest strengths in year two. In year one my excellent relationship with students was noted on a number of separate occasions. Again this continues to be an ongoing trend. 'Excellent relationship with learners and a nice relaxed delivery style.' (Observation 5). 'Good use of praise to encourage and motivate.' (Observation 6). 'Learners were highly motivated; they ask and answer questions well.' (Observation on 7).

This approach is indicative of the humanistic approach to teaching that recognises the learner as an individual. As a teacher I have to develop a degree of flexibility and empathy towards the learner's personal situation and this is reflective in the very positive relationship I have with most of my learners.

This approach to the welfare of students is a theoretical approach noted by Carl Rogers. Rogers within his humanistic theory emphasised the importance of 'unconditional positive regard' – respect and consideration for the individual regardless of their circumstances.

I feel that in all respects this is one of my greatest strengths within teaching – I endeavour to treat all learners as individuals wherever possible. This degree of flexibility allows the students a certain level of autonomy and encourages students to be active participants in their own learning.

Further observation assessments also acknowledge the strengths in terms of the planning and organisation for sessions. 'Well planned session with detailed lesson plan and rationale' (Observation 7) '. . . that clearly links theory to practice.' (Observation 6). This concept is implicit within my personality: I need to feel totally prepared for sessions and am unable to leave teaching to chance.

The role of observations within education allows for a level of accountability. This evaluation, although stressful to the individual teacher, provides an element of accountability within the classroom. 'Students have an interest, too, in knowing that those who teach them are monitored regularly and effectively so that problems and difficulties arising in the classroom are not covered up and ignored.' (Curzon, 2004, p413). Personally, however, I have through internal and external inspection, been observed over 12 times in two years. I feel that there is a critical period whereupon inspection is valuable to the teacher and the organisation, and an amount whereupon the teacher becomes complacent by the process.

I feel that I have grown considerably within the two years and this has been recognised within observation practice within this academic year, 'You bring students back on task well, you are stronger and more assertive.' (Observation 7). 'You adapted your activities to meet the needs of the smaller group which shows flexibility and confidence.' (Observation 6).

I feel really pleased by these comments. I do feel more in control and do not feel the need to teach in such a regimented fashion. If the class deviates a little from the plan but the discussion still allows for learners' development and challenge or to address the learners' knowledge or attitudes, I am more able now to bring them back to task with confidence.

REFLECTIVE TASK

1. Thinking about your first observation, how have you prepared?
2. Does your mentor have any helpful advice?

Best practice in preparing for observed teaching

A good starting point is to run through the basic practical things involved in your observation. Making sure you have addressed all of these will take a lot of the stress out of the experience.

Preparation

1. Make sure you have clearly agreed date, time and venue with your observation tutor/ mentor.
2. Please advise the tutor about any time needed to sign in or park so that the observation can start on time.
3. Please facilitate access to the college/training centre/workshop as necessary, i.e. arrange to meet the tutor or let reception know they are coming.
4. Try to prepare the room so the observer can see you, the learners and the board/ screen/TV, etc. You should have advised the learners that the session will be observed and introduce the observer to your learners. Make sure you have checked all the technology is working before the lesson.
5. If the observation is in a practical workshop you will need to consider health and safety and clothing for the observer. You will also need to discuss their needs in terms of being able to see a range of work and to record your performance with different learners.
6. Complete the pre-observation paperwork and make sure your observer has a copy of this before or during the observation. Your paperwork should clearly reference sources for activities/theories/concepts being used and a justification for their choice. You must include targeting of the New Professional Standards and why you feel these specific targets will be met during the session.

Observation

1. Make sure you are familiar with the criteria that are used on the observation report form. (These are taken from the revised Ofsted framework.) This will help you to work to the best of your ability.
2. Make sure your observer has a copy of the scheme of work/course programme, rationale, lesson plan and a description of the course and cohort. If this description is not normally recorded, it should be done for the observation because it will help your assessment. Other documents would include register and student records, e.g. mark book, value added scores. Provide evidence (as appropriate) of the learners' performance on entry, progress to date, learning plans and targets, etc.
3. Make sure your observer has a copy of the session/lesson plan for the observation and a complete set of any resources such as handouts.

Reflective discussion

1. The observation will usually last 45–60 minutes. Ideally the observer will want to have the reflective discussion straightaway. If 15 minutes can be built into the session (a break, team-teaching, guided study) then please do so. You will need to give some thought to where the meeting can take place, i.e. you may want some privacy.

2. If it is not appropriate or possible to have the meeting straight away, you need to agree with the observer when the meeting will take place. This should take place as soon as possible. Telephone discussion is acceptable in these circumstances. If there is no convenient break, please facilitate the departure of the observer as best as you can.

3. Your observer will structure the meeting to allow for free and frank discussion to take place to enable you to get any support or advice necessary. Your observer will demonstrate the following characteristics during the meeting: they will be supportive, give you advice on how to develop your skills better in the future, be accurate in their assessment and will be a critical friend.

4. Make sure you are clear about the targets for development and that you create an appropriate plan to address them.

5. Complete a self-evaluation of the session. You need to show evidence of critical reflection and insightful evaluation. It is important to be detailed and address all the issues raised during the observation.

6. Ensure you reflect on your observation in your reflective log a week after the event. This will give you a different perspective and enable you to be more impartial and link your thoughts to the theoretical framework.

7. Make sure you put all of the evidence of your observation into your professional development portfolio straight away to ensure nothing gets lost.

Benefits of observed teaching

1. View the reflective discussion as a platform for improvement, not as a criticism of current performance. Remember to complete an evaluation report on the observed session/lesson and to make use of your reflective log. Discuss the session/lesson with your mentor.

2. Aspire to deliver your best session or lesson. Be ambitious, try something new, be innovative. In this way you will find it easier to have ideas and issues to raise in evaluation and reflection, and subsequently share with others, a process from which we will all benefit.

3. You should engage with your observer to ensure clarification of all points raised, especially areas for development. It is also an opportunity to ask for constructive advice where the session has not gone as you wanted. Your observing tutors have seen many lessons and will have ideas to share.

Understanding and achieving LLUK standards

Your teaching observations will provide the vehicle for you to demonstrate your achievement of the professional practice component of the LLUK standards. These standards are achieved by you demonstrating competence under observed conditions of each specific standard.

Due to the variety and number of standards you may not demonstrate them all via observed lessons but may achieve some via micro teaching sessions or by taking part in other activities within your placement organisation.

Wherever the standard is demonstrated it must be observed and signed off by your mentor, your observer or a colleague within your organisation. Failure to demonstrate achievement of all of the standards will result in failure of the programme of study.

As you can see, it is imperative that you make yourself familiar with the LLUK standards and plan your observed sessions in order to maximise the opportunities for you to achieve them. Each standard need only be achieved once but can be demonstrated on more than one occasion.

The identification of which standards are evidenced in each session and the tracking of those achieved is your responsibility. You must be rigorous in your planning and tracking to ensure nothing is missed.

Your mentor will be specifically concerned with signing off those standards that come in Domain C – Specialist learning and teaching. This is an area of vital importance because you must first and foremost be competent in your subject area in order to gain employment and to teach effectively. Your mentor is the expert and will inform the place of study if they feel you are not able to demonstrate sufficient expertise in your subject area.

Your observation tutor will focus on observing your generic teaching skills and use of appropriate teaching and learning strategies.

Throughout your practice you will need to show clear understanding and familiarity with the standards and will need to be able to discuss your rationale for choosing standards to be assessed on.

During your feedback you will need to reflect on the achievement, or not, of those standards. By having a clear understanding you can engage in professional discussion with your observer and will be able to support and justify your choices. An example of a tracking sheet is included in Appendix 3 for your guidance.

Preparing your paperwork

In the previous chapter we discussed the paperwork needed to prepare a good session. This paperwork will vary according to your place of study. However, the quality of that paperwork does not change.

Paperwork should be well prepared, proofread and organised for each session. A pack containing all the relevant paperwork should be given to the observer at the start of the session and your teaching file should be available for inspection.

It is essential that the observer can see all previous observations and evaluations and can make an informed judgement as to whether the targets for development from the previous observations have been met. The grade/outcome of your observation is based not just on what actually takes place during the observation but on your ability to prepare the paperwork, to meet previously set targets and to be able to take part in a professional discussion to justify your choices of teaching and learning strategies.

CASE STUDY

The observation experience of Chris – training to teach English/media

Since my initial observation, graded 'satisfactory', I have sourced information, guidance and support from colleagues, mentors and observers to improve my professional practice. This has seen my teaching observations consistently achieve a grade two 'good' with the occasional grade one 'outstanding' being awarded.

During my two years' teaching practice, I have felt increasingly more confident in the classroom and in front of learners. My sessions are thoroughly planned and well resourced, giving me an excellent base to teach from.

I am fully aware of the techniques that I choose to implement, that they are appropriate and that they have a positive effect on my learners. I select teaching activities that are relevant to the needs of my learners and will adapt them to suit my needs. I try to utilise different methods of learning and teaching to enhance my sessions and to give my learners the best possible classroom experience.

While I have now become a specialist in the post-compulsory sector, I also believe I have become a specialist in education within my organisation. In discussions with colleagues I often need to explain methods of teaching and learning, how they are relevant and why I have chosen to use them.

I feel I have learnt and developed personally and professionally through the observation process and am genuinely enthused with my future opportunities. I feel that my experiences in teaching accompanied by my academic achievement will give me an excellent background to enable me to deliver high-quality courses that will meet the needs and demands of my students.

PRACTICAL TASK PRACTICAL TASK **PRACTICAL TASK** PRACTICAL TASK **PRACTICAL TASK**

1. Read through the LLUK standards and identify approximately five that you think you can achieve in your first observation.
2. Produce a clear rationale for your choice of each standard.

Making sense of your observation report

Your observer will produce a written report for you about the session they have observed. This will vary in format depending on your place of study but will be detailed and will contain clear indications of the areas that went well during the observation and the areas on which you need to work before the next observation.

An example of an observation report is included in Appendix 4 to give you an idea of the type of written feedback you can expect.

What to expect from your feedback

As discussed earlier in the chapter, the feedback you receive from your observer is crucial. It is important that you try to remember as much as possible of the verbal feedback, so don't be afraid to take notes. Do question your observer and ask for clarification of any areas that you are not sure about.

You should expect a face-to-face 'professional discussion' or 'feedback' meeting after each observation and this should take place as soon as possible. At this meeting you should be given a copy of the observation report and the grade/outcome of the observation.

Your observer should then discuss the session with you, giving clear pointers for future improvement and asking you to justify your choices of activities and assessment tasks.

This is a two-way process and you can question the observer's opinions and decisions if you think anything has been missed or misinterpreted.

Make the most of this meeting as you will need to reflect on it in your professional development journal/diary and you will need include the feedback in your evaluation of the session.

Action planning for future development

After you have completed your feedback meeting you need to complete an evaluation of the whole observation process. This should be critically reflective and should make appropriate links between theory and practice and reference quotes appropriately. By identifying the strengths and areas for improvement in the session you will be able to compile an action plan for your professional development.

This action plan can form part of an existing action plan or can be specifically as a result of this observation and should include clear identification of how you are going to address the observer-set targets from your observation report as well as any you yourself have identified.

Your action points should be SMART and should identify a clear timeframe in which they are going to be addressed.

Example action plan

Priority	Action	Reason	Process	Deadline
1	Consider the appropriateness of the card activity for your group of adult students	Adult students found the card activity lacking in challenge and a bit patronising	Identify an alternative strategy/activity to achieve the same outcome	End of term 1
2	Ensure equal opportunities are considered when designing scenarios	One of the scenarios used was a little controversial and students from some backgrounds may be uncomfortable discussing this issue	Replace the problem scenario with an alternative that ensures equality	End of term 2
3	Clarify the distinction between social costs and environmental costs to ensure students have a clear understanding	Not all students could demonstrate a clear understanding of the difference between the two	Produce a handout to clarify and use in the recap	End of term 2

A SUMMARY OF **KEY POINTS**

In this chapter we have:

> explored the rationale for the observation of teaching and learning;

> discussed the role of feedback in improving your own practice;

> considered the issues action planning for future improvement;

> identified strategies that can be used in planning for observed sessions.

REFERENCES REFERENCES REFERENCES REFERENCES REFERENCES REFERENCES

Curzon, LB (2004) *Teaching in Further Education. An outline of principles and practice* (sixth edition). London: Continuum.

Goleman, D (2005) *Emotional Intelligence.* London: Bantam Books.

Office for Standards in Education (2004) *Framework for the Inspection of Initial Training of Further Education Teachers.* HMI 2274. London: Ofsted Publications.

Russell, T (1998) *Effective Feedback Skills.* London: Kogan Page.

Smart, JK (2003) *Real Coaching and Feedback.* Harlow: Prentice-Hall.

FURTHER READING FURTHER READING FURTHER READING FURTHER READING

Cooze, A (2006) *100 Ideas for Trainee Teachers.* London: Continuum.

Race, P and Pickford, R (2007) *Making Teaching Work.* London: Sage.

Jocelyn Robson (2008) *Teacher Professionalism in Further and Higher Education*. Routledge
   This book focuses on professionalism, professional standards and the nature of professionalism within the workplace. It provides an interesting overview of the developments within the industry and the role of teachers within it.

Steward, A (2006) *FE Lecturer's Survival Guide.* London: Continuum.

Susan Wallace (2007) *Teaching, Tutoring and Training*. Learning Matters
   This book is good because it focuses on specific issues that occur in the lifelong learning sector and is full of useful hints and tips. This is particularly useful for people new to teaching.

Websites

Department for Children, Schools and Families
   www.dcsf.gov.uk
Department for Innovation, Universities and Skills
   www.dius.gov.uk
Learning and Skills Network
   www.lsneducation.org.uk
Success for All
   www.successforall.gov.uk
Teachernet
   www.teachernet.gov.uk/

4
Reflecting on your own practice

The objectives of this chapter

This chapter is designed to provide you with a clear picture of the role of reflection in your teaching and how you can utilise and develop this skill in order to enhance your practice. It will provide a framework which makes clear links between your subject specialism, your teaching and current theory to help you to fully develop dual professionalism.

It addresses the following professional practice standards for QTLS:

AP 4.2 Reflect on and demonstrate commitment to improvement of own personal and teaching skills through regular evaluation and feedback.

BP 2.6 Evaluate the efficiency and effectiveness of own teaching, including consideration of learner feedback and learning theories.

DP 3.1 Evaluate the success of planned learning activities.

Introduction

Endless drama clouds consciousness.
Too much noise overwhelms the senses.
Continual input obscures genuine insight.
Do not substitute sensationalism for learning.
Allow regular time for silent reflection. Turn inward and digest what happened. Let the senses rest and grow still.
When people have time to reflect, they can see more clearly what is essential in themselves and others.

Adapted from Heider, J (1999, p23) *Time for Reflection*

When considering 'reflection' a good starting point is to define what reflection is and why it is considered important in your teaching role. When thinking of the word 'reflection' what may spring to mind is your face reflecting back in the mirror. Take for example when you last brushed your teeth in front of the mirror. As you looked at your reflection there was a conscious awareness of what you were doing. Like the recognition of your face in the mirror, reflection is a mental process which offers a way to learn from direct experience rather than second-hand, e.g through books.

This is known as experiential learning because it is based on real-life experiences and has a direct impact in this context on your learners. Reflections help to develop your awareness of what you already know and importantly identify any gaps you may need to address.

If you think about a day of your teaching practice you may go from one lesson to the next, superficially reflecting whether it went well or not and resolving to do things differently next time. It is important to harness these thoughts and to revisit them as soon as you can in order to learn from them. These deeper reflections allow a probing into why it went well, what can be improved and what can be transferred to other sessions or situations. From this knowledge you can begin to build up a range of strategies and techniques that can be used and adapted in order to improve your teaching and professional development continuously.

Reflection is about more than building up knowledge. It is about examining how that knowledge can be applied to your teaching practice in a meaningful way. It is important to adopt a controlled approach to your reflection in which you take ownership of exactly how, where and when you reflect and determine clear actions to improve your practice in future.

Reflection

Human self-reflection is the capacity of humans to exercise introspection and the willingness to learn more about our fundamental nature, purpose and essence. Boud defines this as

> *an important human activity in which people recapture their experience, think about it, mull it over and evaluate it. It is working with experience that is important in learning*

(Boud, 1985, p124)

Reflective practice

'Reflective practice' is a term often used in education pedagogy. It is a continuous process from a personal perspective that considers critical incidents within your life's experiences.

Reflective practice involves thoughtfully considering one's own experiences in applying theory to practice. In teacher education it refers to the process of trainees studying their own teaching methods and determining what works best for the students. All lecturers need to reflect on their experiences in the classroom and adapt their strategies accordingly.

> *By reflecting critically, instead of continuing with our feelings of self doubt, we can become positive in our search for new understandings of our practice and more ways to deal with the challenges that confront us continually. We take control over our professional practice, acknowledging that we cannot transform everything, but aware that we can identify the spheres in which we can. It is a truly emancipatory process.*

(Hillier, 2005, p20)

Reflection can take place at different stages during or/and after the lessons. The stages of reflection may be as depicted in Figure 4.1.

Figure 4.1 Stages of reflection

Description: What happened?

Evaluation: Did your lesson go well?

Analysis: What are your feelings and thoughts? What could you have done better to make the lesson more dynamic? Was the lesson too long? Do you need to increase your teaching and learning strategies? On the other hand, what made the lesson work so well? Do you need to continue to use Q&A techniques? Did they really engage the students?

Action: What are your next steps to aid development of your classroom practice? Are the resources fit for purpose? How will you change them?

REFLECTIVE TASK

1. Using this model, consider one of your lessons and reflect on your performance. How does this model work for you?
2. Are there any other areas you might want to include in your own reflections?

Kolb (1984) offers a useful cyclical model for reflecting on each stage of your teaching and learning (Figure 4.2).

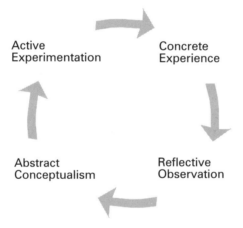

Figure 4.2 Kolb's learning cycle (Kolb, 1984)

When looking at this model and exploring your classroom practice there is one key factor which will shape your action and lead your journey around the cycle. The essential component is how you position the student in your definitions and classroom practice.

The student is the person who will learn, the person who arrives into the educational setting with thoughts, feelings and opinions of their own. As such it is important to remember that the student is not a blank sheet of paper but an individual who brings with them life experiences. In order to address the 'whole person' you need to reflect on your students' attitudes, experiences, knowledge and how they will shape the way you deliver your lessons By forging a relationship with the learners and gaining knowledge of the whole person, you can begin to reflect on teaching and learning strategies and how these can be adapted to meet your learners' needs.

Your reflective diary

While you are undertaking your teacher training programme you will be asked to keep a reflective diary or journal. This journal will vary in both size and format depending on your place of study but will have common components.

It is essential that you keep regular reflections of your progress and that these are considered, insightful and critical and not just descriptions of your lessons. You must ensure that you reflect upon your teaching, your learning, your engagement with your mentor, critical incidents during your programme and anything else that impacts upon your development as a deliverer of post-compulsory education and training. Your reflections should be clearly linked to the theory and referenced appropriately. It is important that your reflections are critical and evaluative and consider issues in depth.

You should include at least one entry that reflects upon each of:

- assessment and feedback to learners;
- behaviour;
- inclusivity/access;
- individual target setting/personalised learning;
- communication strategies;
- your specialist area.

There should be clear evidence of the growth and development of your skills in reflection throughout the programme, with more attention being given to linking theory to practice in the later part of the programme. You should demonstrate understanding of this growth in your reflections and demonstrate your independence, by deciding what to reflect upon and in what depth.

Another good technique to use when reflecting is to structure your writing using the following framework.

- Brief description.
- What went well?
- Why?
- Even better if...
- Why?
- What the theory has to say.
- Your own conclusions.

CASE STUDY
Mel – Training to teach small-animal care
My first lesson

During my first lesson I felt understandably nervous; it was very well planned and I had prepared a very detailed PowerPoint presentation with pictures and activities. This enabled me to structure the session and to engage the students in their learning.

Vizard (2007) explains how crucial first impressions are. He says that the impact you make during the first few minutes when you meet a group is critical. As I spoke from my PowerPoint as if it were a script I feel that my first impression was dull and predictable (Brookfield, 1990, p79). In the future I will use skeleton notes as recommended by Brookfield; these are drawn up and depict an ordered and systematic progression of ideas, but have the advantage of allowing me the freedom to digress and to include personal anecdotes, when these seem appropriate. Also it is easier to respond to questions, as I can respond more quickly and confidently without getting confused.

REFLECTIVE TASK

1. Using this model, reflect on one of your teaching sessions
2. What areas for development do you identify?

Other tips

- Keep a notebook with you so you can note down your reflections at any time. It's surprising how ideas can pop up when we least expect.
- Remember, you do not have to show anyone your reflections, so be honest. If you need to, ask your tutor or mentor for input.
- Listen to the voices of your learners, include their ideas and feelings in your reflections.
- Don't be too hard on yourself. Celebrate what you can do, as well as what you would like to develop.

Linking theory to practice

The idea of linking theory to practice can initially be a barrier for trainees. The challenge lies in justifying what you are doing, what you may do naturally in your classroom practice, and linking this to the ideas of others.

An essential part of your development as a teacher is to be open to the ideas of others, including your tutors, mentor, other teachers and your learners. This needs to be securely underpinned by a thorough knowledge of current theory and any research published in your chosen field. It would be naive to expect to be able to teach 'perfectly' from the start, or to be able to 'know' what to do in all situations without reference to other people's ideas and advice.

Reading is an essential requirement of the programme of study you are on and you need to read widely in order to access the variety of material available to support your development in the classroom. At the end of the chapter you will find a list of recommended reading. However, there is such a variety of published material that it is easy to find a wide range of books that will enable you to inform your own practice and link with your reflective accounts.

Choosing the right passages to support your own reflections may take some time and may involve access to a number of books, so you may need to do this after the event. However, it is recommended that you buy some core textbooks and be prepared to supplement this selection when faced with a particular issue or concern.

CASE STUDY
Mel – Training to teach small-animal care
Group work
When putting students into groups for activities in future, I will split the class into at least four or six groups, so that they have time to work on their answers and be able to discuss them quietly between just a few of their peers, allowing more individual input. Smaller groups are probably better than large ones due to the weaker members being able to 'hide' in larger groups (Reece, I and Walker, S. 2007, p103). This should allow members of the group to have much more input. Group members get more immediate feedback for their contributions. They are more likely to feel involved and satisfied with what they are doing. Active, dynamic learning is possible because of the high level of involvement (Malouf, 2003, p75). I may perhaps get them to work on the tasks outside of their friendship groups (Vizard, 2007). This may improve their communication skills and they won't just rely on their friends or have distracting conversations. However, well-established relationships and roles may lead to more efficient use of time. I may try to get them to work in their friendship groups one week and separate them the next week to see what works best. I may find that it changes with different groups I teach, and different levels.

REFLECTIVE TASK

1. Consider a situation where you have used group work. Did you plan the groups before the lesson? Did it work?
2. What would you do differently in future?

Reflecting on critical incidents

It is important that alongside your regular reflections you also reflect on any critical incidents that occur during your teaching experience. A critical incident is an event that occurs that you did not expect and that has a profound effect on your teaching or on the learning of students. A critical incident is not necessarily a major event but it is an event that changes your thinking and your future practice.

Sometimes small incidents are critical in making us adjust our thinking and in allowing us to see the big picture. We can get very focused on the day-to-day business of lesson planning and teaching. Sometimes it takes a critical incident to make us stop, focus and consider the overall effectiveness of our practice.

As teachers in the Lifelong Learning Sector we have a responsibility to do our very best both inside and outside the classroom and in order to do this we need to be able to see the big picture and to reflect on our own progress towards our overall goals.

CASE STUDY
Graham – training to teach sport
Equality and diversity
While researching for an assignment I read the following question from Wallace, who

asks, *Have measures been taken to ensure that teaching materials (books, handouts, film, video, etc.) do not contain sexist stereotyping?* (Wallace, 2007, p123).

This prompted me to evaluate my own practice and to realise that I was guilty of using a very narrow range of images in my presentations.

I undertook to investigate a range of PowerPoint backgrounds. I now have a personal compilation of more than 500 templates which are sports-specific, many of which promote minority sports. They include images of female performers and other minority groups including disabilities and ethnic minorities.

These PowerPoint templates have been shared with my team to ensure that we are all maintaining the highest standards of professional practice.

We can see this is a critical incident in Graham's development and that he has sensibly used reflection to change his teaching practice.

PRACTICAL TASK PRACTICAL TASK PRACTICAL TASK PRACTICAL TASK PRACTICAL TASK

1. Look back through all your resources and reflect on your use of images – are they inclusive?
2. Research on the internet for sources of alternative images.

Developing your critical thinking

No need is more fundamentally human than our need to understand the meaning of our experience.

(Jack Mezirow, 1990, p11)

Critical reflection offers you the opportunity to deconstruct your prior assumptions such as beliefs, attitudes, value systems, and social emotion in a rational way.

Learning from experience is one of the aims of critical reflection. It is known as experiential learning. Brookfield (1995) noted that adults are capable of learning through critical reflection. Indeed, in today's workplaces where we are often extremely busy with workloads, learning from experience is an extremely valuable skill. Reflection allows you to have a focused thought. You can focus on why/how you have responded to a situation and develop and apply your learning in new situations, e.g. a new group of learners, a different curriculum level. Reflection offers a way for you to learn from your direct experiences, rather than from the experiences of others. This can make it more meaningful and give it a stronger impact.

Critical reflection allows you to identify the problems in a situation within your teaching. Such situations become a context from which you can learn and develop your skills in the classroom.

Critical reflection is a firm feature in adult education, relevant to yourself as a practitioner and to your learners. Critically reflecting allows insights into experiences which can lead to the integration and application of new knowledge into other situations. It is therefore important that as a trainee and in your future position as a professional in lifelong learning, critical reflection should underpin your practice.

To maximise your learning through reflection you will need to position yourself firmly at the heart of the experience. In this context, theory, knowledge and experience provide a mattress to understand and critically uncover the experience in different ways.

At the centre of Mezirow's theory of adult education is the concept of transformative or transformational learning. This theory clearly recognises that the development of new knowledge or change in currently held assumptions/perspectives through critical reflection may result in a dramatic change in the meanings we place on situations. Vitally, the learning process requires more than adding new knowledge to what is already known. Rather, the new learning transforms the previous knowledge into a new perspective, enabling the learner to increase their world view and challenge current beliefs.

Moon (2000) identified five phases in the learning process shifting the learner from 'surface' learning to transformative learning. Reflection in the transformative learning phase facilitates the learner to critically examine and collate greater understanding of a situation, self, or his or her knowledge (Moon). When you engage in critical reflection you have to have enough evidence to recognise and accept the validity of the new concept and to change its meaning, perspectives or schemes. Through this developmental process, you can leave behind previous assumptions and become a critical thinker and autonomous learner.

To be a truly reflective practitioner and to continue to grow and learn from your teaching, you need to be critically reflective and to identify and implement changes to your existing practice. You must continue this practice even after your teacher training is complete because outstanding teachers must be adaptive and constantly changing their practice to meet the changing needs of their learners and the industry in which they work.

Transformational learning and critical reflection can be just as profound after 20 years of teaching as they are in your first year. It is imperative that you are aware that it is not just your students who are lifelong learners. You yourself will be a lifelong learner for as long as you want to be an outstanding teacher.

CASE STUDY
Angela – training to teach health and social care
Critical thinking

I had assumed that a second-year level 3 group would have quite well developed research skills, particularly given that they were young learners (17–20 years old) and very conversant with technology. However, they were not creative in their thinking and found it difficult, during the group work, to make and follow links between global, national and individual issues. I was quite frustrated that new concepts did not emerge during their consideration of the issues but had to be spoon-fed to them by me.

I think there were two strands to this problem. The first was to do with the students' prior experiences of learning which is perhaps best summed up by Heraclitus who said *He who does not expect the unexpected will not detect it: for him it will remain undetectable and unapproachable* (cited in Curzon, 2004, p89). Curzon (2004) adds that the potential for creative thinking often goes unrealised in students and this is because they are encouraged, whether intentionally or unintentionally, to accept knowledge and instruction uncritically. If I am to try to change this behaviour it will be important for me to encourage students to restructure and experiment with information in order that problem-solving can occur.

This leads to the second strand of the problem which is that, perhaps due to lack of prior knowledge of the group, I had not adequately arranged the lesson so that discovery of patterns and solutions was successfully enabled.

Gestalt psychology points to the teacher to facilitate the finding of a route to the solution of the problem and also the need for learners to be aware that their efforts should be aimed in that direction (Curzon, 2004). On reflection, I feel that I should have done some preliminary activities first in order to prepare the ground for the research activity and point learners in the right direction. Perhaps putting the video, which I had scheduled near the end of the session, nearer to the beginning, would have provided the direction that the students did not have. This would have provided the learners with increasingly structured insight, eventually leading to the level of understanding I had hoped they would gain.

PRACTICAL TASK PRACTICAL TASK PRACTICAL TASK PRACTICAL TASK PRACTICAL TASK

1. Identify an incident in one of your lessons and write a critical reflection, make sure you consider all aspects of the incident and how you may adapt your practice in the future.
2. Show this to your mentor and ask for some feedback.

CASE STUDY

Amy – training to teach dance

Since I was a little girl I have always had a real passion for dance. Even though I achieved my GCSEs in maths and English I knew that I didn't want to pursue them further. However, I was good at dance and in this knowledge knew that continuing with it would not only make me happy – but it could also be my future career. So it was with big dreams that I headed to a school of dance and then returned to Southport to complete my studies.

After my studies I worked as a professional dancer in local and national productions; it was fantastic. I was me when I was on stage and this gave me a confidence that I wanted to share with others. This sharing was the motivation for me becoming a teacher. It's about passing on the skills I'd developed, but much more than that, allowing others to explore the rhythm inside their own body and the confidence this instils.

I started teaching dance, aerobics, Pilates, salsa – aerobics and aqua aerobics. My students were 18–80 each of them attending for their own reasons. The lady who was 80 wanted to grab her dream before it was too late. The girl, who put her first pair of ballet shoes on, had the same dreams but with a life ahead of her she told me how she pictured herself on a huge stage surrounded by eyes and applause. Each one of the pupils I connected with and shared their hopes and their aspirations.

It was this passion that drove me to commence the Cert Ed in HE programme. Of course I was nervous, I knew my subject but as teaching and learning theories began to be explored I found it hard going. I questioned what reflection had to do with teaching – surely dance was in the here and now – catching the moment. So why reflect?

However, as I began to explore different strategies to meet the needs of my learners – music for the auditory, props for the kinesthaetic, a screen with splashes and colour for the visual learner – I began to reflect on my practice and importantly how to develop it.

Armitage et al (2003, p41) suggest *Perhaps the greatest tool which will lead to your development as a teacher is self evaluation.*

Rather than letting a weak lesson slide by, where not all the learners had been engaged I'd ask why was this? What could I have done to hold their attention? I'd look at my lesson plan, look at the assessment strategies, content of the lesson – what was missing? By critically reflecting I was able to transform my strategies so that the learners' needs were met.

For example – a key aspect of my practice which really developed through reflection was the need to differentiate. This meant ensuring that I challenged the top end of the group but importantly also challenged and included the learners who struggled. From the reflection my communication skills needed to develop specifically in relation to my questioning and answering techniques.

I'd use the meta-language of dance and performance assuming the learners would understand. Some did but others grew silent and withdrawn from discussions. Some would distract the lesson to stop me pursuing questions. When I read my feedback forms the reason came to light. They were baffled by the some of the language I used. It made them feel 'stupid' when they not only did not understand it but watched others in the group answer so clearly.

As a result of this I simplified the language and gave the group definition sheets so they could develop their language acquisition skills. As the weeks progressed I built in more complex language but always after I'd introduced it earlier. This not only facilitated the meta-language development of the group but also helped them to express themselves succinctly when they were writing essays and importantly when they attended interviews.

Reflection helped me to see the bigger picture of my practice – not just the dance steps, the moves – but how the information could be processed and put into action by the learners. I also realised that learning is a two-way process – not only did I teach the learners but they taught me – this sharing of knowledge was truly liberating.

REFLECTIVE TASK

1. Consider Amy's experience and identify any critical incidents she has encountered.
2. How do you think she has changed her practice as a result of these critical incidents?

A SUMMARY OF **KEY POINTS**

In this chapter we have:

> **emphasised the importance of reflective practice in linking theory to practice;**

> **discussed the role of your reflective diary in developing your teaching and achieving your teaching qualification;**

> **explored the issues of transformational learning and critical reflection in teaching;**

> **considered the reflections of other trainee teachers and their experiences.**

REFERENCES REFERENCES REFERENCES REFERENCES REFERENCES

Armitage, A et al (2007) *Teaching and Training in Post Compulsory Education*. Buckingham: Open University Press.

Brookfield, S (1995) Adult Learning: An Overview. In A. Tuinjman (ed.) *International Encyclopedia of Education.* Oxford: Pergammon Press.

Boud, D (1985) *Reflection: Turning Experience into Learning*. Abingdon: Routledge-Falmer.

Curzon, LB (2004) *Teaching in Further Education. An outline of principles and practice.* (sixth edition). London: Continuum.

Hillier, Y (2005) *Reflective Teaching in Further and Adult Education.* London: Continuum.

Kolb, D (1984) *Experiential Learning: Experience as the Source of Learning and Development*. Englewood Cliffs: Prentice-Hall.

Malouf, D (2005) *How to Teach Adults in a Fun and Exciting Way.* London: Allen & Unwin.

Mezirow, J et.al (1990) *Fostering Critical Reflection in Adulthood.* San Francisco, CA: Jossey-Bass.

Moon, JA (2000) *Reflection in Learning and Professional Development: Theory and Practice.* London: Kogan Page.

Reece, I and Walker, S (2007) *Teaching, Training and Learning.* Tyne & Wear: Business Education Publishers.

Vizard, D (2007) *How to Manage Behaviour in Further Education.* London: Sage.

Wallace, S (2007) *Teaching, Tutoring and Training in the Lifelong Learning Sector.* Exeter: Learning Matters.

FURTHER READING FURTHER READING FURTHER READING FURTHER READING

Brookfield, S (1995) Adult Learning: An Overview. In A Tuinjman (ed.) *International Encyclopedia of Education.* Oxford: Pergamon Press.

Jodi Roffey-Barentsen and Richard Malthouse (2009) *Reflective Practice in the Lifelong Learning Sector*. Learning Matters

This book is a valuable introduction to reflection and gives some realistic advice and includes examples of reflective accounts from practitioners in the Lifelong Learning Sector.

Mezirow, J et al (1990) *Fostering Critical Reflection in Adulthood.* San Francisco, CA: Jossey-Bass.

Moon, J (1999) *Learning Journals: A Handbook for Academics, Students and Professional Development*. London: Kogan Page.

Moon, JA (2000) *Reflection in Learning and Professional Development: Theory and Practice.* London: Kogan Page.

Yvonne Hillier (2005) *Reflective Teaching in Further and Adult Education*. Continuum

Hillier's book identifies the importance of reflection in our teaching and how this impacts on our development into outstanding teachers. It contains a mixture of theory and practical advice and tips for teachers.

Websites

LLUK
www.lluk.org
Office for Standards in Education
www.ofsted.gov.uk
QCA
www.qca.org.uk
Standards Agency
www.standards.dfes.gov.uk

5
What to expect from your mentor

The objectives of this chapter

This chapter is designed to provide you with some guidance on what to expect from your mentor during your placement whether you are part-time, full-time, pre-service or in-service. It includes advice on preparation for observations, on structuring your weekly meetings and on receiving constructive feedback following your observed teaching sessions with your mentor. Key to this chapter is advice on establishing a professional working relationship with your mentor.

> As with many of the roles that support experiential learning, it succeeds or fails on the basis of the relationship that is established between the mentor and the mentee.

> (Fry et al, 1999, p145, in Cunningham, 2005, p30)

This chapter also addresses the following professional practice standards for QTLS:

AS 4 Reflection and evaluation of their own practice and their continuing professional development as teachers.

CS 3 Fulfilling the statutory responsibilities associated with own specialist area.

CK 4.1 Ways to keep up to date with development in teaching in own specialist area.

> Subject-specific skills must be acquired in the trainees' workplace and from vocational or academic experience. Mentoring in related curriculum areas is essential.

> (DfES, 2005)

Introduction

So what constitutes a good mentor? Here is a very useful definition.

> Mentors in PCET are skilled, experienced teachers who are involved in guiding, counselling and supporting trainees in practical ways. They are able to offer both a role model and essential information on a college's learners, its curriculum, its organisational structure and its policies, at least those relating to learning and teaching.

> (Cunningham, 2005, p25)

A significant part of your training is related to the concept of 'dual professionalism'. In other words, not only should you have high-level generic teaching knowledge and skills, but also high-level subject-specific knowledge and skills in order to fulfil the LLUK standards for QTLS.

Such knowledge is never static so it is essential that you keep abreast of all current issues relating to your subject area. Of course you are very much encouraged to do this by research, i.e. reading, attending conferences, being involved in meetings, but the subject-specific mentor is someone who can really help you enhance your knowledge and skills and of course your experiences while on placement. He or she will observe you four times throughout your training and will consistently measure your performance against the new

LLUK professional standards for teachers in PCET, particularly those in Domain C (Specialist Learning and Teaching).

So in this chapter we will consider the main aspects of the mentoring experience, which are:

- induction and shadowing;
- weekly discussions;
- planning for observations;
- supportive lesson observation and feedback;
- a focus on further development.

Therefore there are two key players on your placement: the visiting/supervising tutor and the mentor. It might be worth revisiting Chapter 3 at this point to summarise the observation process.

There are two types of observer: subject-specific mentors and observation tutors. Subject-specific mentors carry out four observations over the length of the programme and concentrate their observations on the accuracy of the trainee's subject knowledge and their ability to convey this to their learners.

In order to encourage consistency of feedback and to provide clear evidence to support grading decisions/outcomes, standard documentation is used and in many organisations observations are graded using the Ofsted grading criteria shown below:

Grade 1 – Outstanding
Grade 2 – Good
Grade 3 – Satisfactory
Grade 4 – Unsatisfactory

All observations must be graded/deemed satisfactory or better to pass your training.

Induction and shadowing

As soon as you start your placement your mentor will be on hand to advise and guide you through the college/institution's procedures and processes. Here is an appropriate list of activities associated with induction and shadowing.

Mentors may provide:

- a plan of the institution; timetable; staff who's who; car parking; dress code;
- an introduction to the department or area and its systems (ordering equipment, coffee club), policies, e.g. disciplinary and marking, health and safety (the staff handbook or copies for trainees would be helpful), syllabuses and resources.

And your mentor:

- should introduce you to learners as a new teacher and not as a student;
- should give you an opportunity to observe a range of teaching;
- should try to help you to recognise key events in lessons and why you have done certain things by being explicit about your actions – this might take place in pre- and post-lesson discussion and can be referred to as sharing your practice.

Remember:

- you may act as a classroom assistant to the mentor and other teachers;
- you should be given specific student information about the classes you are to observe/teach as appropriate, e.g. special needs, disability.

And your mentor:

- Should allocate you some space each day to allow you to reflect on your experiences.

Also:

- you should be given time to talk to/shadow the other members of the institutional workforce.

So while you are shadowing your mentor and other members of the placement institution, it is crucial that you embark on this in a well-prepared way and that you know exactly what to be looking for. Simply put, to watch someone without knowing what to look for is a fruitless activity, however entertaining and pleasant it may seem. You need to really look at what is going on and one very good way to do that is to look at what is expected of trainees in terms of LLUK standards and Ofsted grading criteria.

Mentors have a key role in assessing trainee teachers against the standards, particularly with regard to subject-specific teaching. To ensure standardisation of judgements in observations all mentors and visiting tutors will benchmark decisions against the Ofsted grade criteria in mentor training events led by experienced observers familiar with Ofsted standards.

See **www.ofsted.gov.uk** for what inspectors look for in outstanding trainees, good trainees and satisfactory trainees. For Domain C: Specialist Learning and Teaching standards, please see **www.lluk.org/documents/professional_standards_for_itts020107pdf**

Remember

Trainees will be judged inadequate if they do not meet all of the criteria for the 'satisfactory' standard and have not demonstrated effective achievement of the new overarching professional standards for teachers, tutors in PCET (Ofsted, 2008).

Once you have looked through this information on grading and on the subject-specific standards, you will be instantly armed with what to look for as you can see what an Ofsted inspector is looking for, too.

PRACTICAL TASK PRACTICAL TASK PRACTICAL TASK PRACTICAL TASK

1. Look carefully at the LLUK standards Domain C CP1.1-CP4.2.Choose just a couple of them and comment on to what extent your mentor/observed teacher is addressing these standards in the classroom.
2. Look at the Grade Descriptors at **www.ofsted.co.uk**. Which ones actually describe what you are seeing while you observe classes during your shadowing phase?

After a few observations you will soon realise that there are many ways in which the standards can be met and the quality of how they are met can be measured against the Ofsted criteria.

Weekly discussions with your mentor

Apart from your four observed sessions, your mentor will spend at least one hour per week with you to provide subject specific support and to help you with your reflections which you should log on a weekly basis. Here is an appropriate template you might like to use.

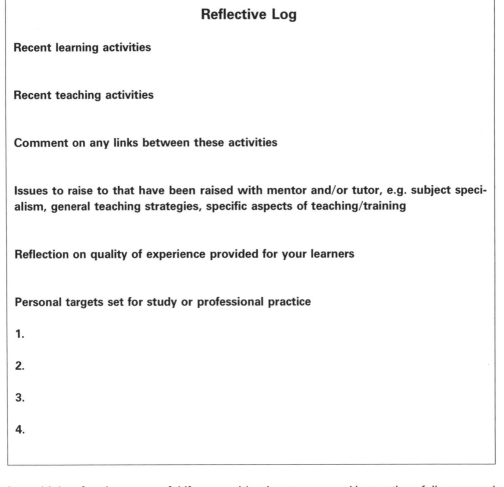

Reflective Log

Recent learning activities

Recent teaching activities

Comment on any links between these activities

Issues to raise to that have been raised with mentor and/or tutor, e.g. subject specialism, general teaching strategies, specific aspects of teaching/training

Reflection on quality of experience provided for your learners

Personal targets set for study or professional practice

1.

2.

3.

4.

It would therefore be very useful if you could arrive at your weekly meetings fully prepared with some points to raise in your discussion. You will be surprised how many questions can arise as part of your everyday activities. Often the most seemingly mundane of events can be a wonderful source of discussion. It is very likely and completely usual that you may have anxieties during your initial phase of the placement particularly and these can be ironed out in your discussion. Here are some typical anxieties experienced by trainees suggested by Cunningham (2005, p28).

- Being assessed and graded.
- Teaching groups of mixed ability and motivation.
- Not being sufficiently knowledgeable.
- Standing in front of a full room of people.
- Finding time for preparation.

- Not being able to answer questions from students.
- Creating interest and a stimulating, animated classroom environment from dry, theoretical subject matter.
- Does it get easier?

CASE STUDY

Mentoring and initial shadowing experience of Andrew

My mentor was very committed to helping me throughout my course, particularly in terms of answering any questions I had which sometimes I felt were a bit trivial or showed my ignorance. However, he was extremely understanding and was able to put himself in my shoes, as it were. During the initial shadowing period I needed to get to grips with what now seem like little things, i.e. timetable, department policies, course specifications and where/when to meet, etc. Then as the observations began I realised I had even more questions on curriculum subject matters, teaching and learning strategies, differentiation, etc. He was extremely busy, teaching up to 24 hours per week. I had been told about the PCET contractual obligations in one of my modules but to experience it first hand was a real eye opener. Yet he always found time to see me and I valued that.

So we can see that first impressions and positive initial experiences are crucial in the mentoring process and are an excellent premise to build on in order to form a fulfilling professional relationship.

Supportive lesson observation and practice

Once your initial shadowing period is over (usually about four weeks) you will enter a developmental phase where your mentor will accompany you when you begin to teach your classes (or at least the mentor will be nearby). Here is a summary of what the developmental phase could entail. (Remember, if you have concerns during this period you can call directly upon your personal tutor to help.)

- Your mentor should provide opportunities for you to discuss issues which are likely to include departmental schemes of work, lesson planning and ordering equipment (including health and safety items), classroom management, behaviour and discipline, developing subject knowledge and ICT skills and marking.
- You may actually assist the mentor and other colleagues in their teaching, e.g. working with groups, supporting activities, acting as an extra pair of hands and eyes.
- You should be involved in planning and collaborative teaching with the mentor.
- 'Flying solo'. At first this is likely to involve the mentor/colleague being present during the lesson, but as deemed appropriate this 'support' could withdraw to 'nearby', i.e. the effect of the teacher in the room is removed but help is at hand if necessary. A suggestion here is that really you should not be teaching any more than four hours per three-day period.
- Your mentor will provide supportive lesson observation and feedback.

Your mentor should now provide time to discuss issues which focus on your individual needs identified during the initial shadowing. This is likely to include further development of subject knowledge and ICT skills, assessment including levelling and target setting, investigations and differentiation as well as planning and classroom management.

Remember you will have four observations from your mentor and these will be evenly spread over the period of training so that you can indeed measure your development. So don't be daunted too much by the prospect of your first full observation by your mentor. Look upon it as an opportunity to learn even if it is to learn by making mistakes.

There is no one way to teach any class. You will have your LLUK standards, grading criteria, your lesson plan and rationale and of course your subject knowledge. Plan your observations carefully. Revisit Chapter 3 of this book and make sure you are prepared.

After your observations, your mentor will offer constructive feedback which will consist of strengths and targets. What follows is a comprehensive guide to giving and receiving feedback and a suggested format for carrying it out after an observation.

Receiving and giving professional feedback

Feedback is the process of offering observations (usually oral and written) about performance, seeking to identify strengths and areas for development so that you are able to build on their strengths and develop your weaker areas.

Feedback may be oral or written, and can be constructive – encouraging and supportive – or destructive – too negative.

Constructive feedback increases self-awareness, offers options and encourages development, so it can be important to give and receive it. Constructive feedback does not mean only favourable feedback. Critical and challenging feedback, given skilfully, is very important and useful in the development of the learner.

Destructive feedback means feedback that is given in an unskilled or negative way and leaves the recipient simply feeling bad, with seemingly nothing on which to build, with no options for using the learning experience to aid development.

When giving feedback, it is important always to keep in mind that the purpose of the feedback is to help the recipient to improve and develop and that this is most likely to be achieved by a careful balance of two ingredients, namely support and challenge.

Support means identifying, praising and reinforcing success, offering encouragement, making practical suggestions, recognising difficulties and suggesting routes through or around them. This supports the learner's self-esteem, because effort and success have been recognised.

Challenge means pushing someone's thinking, prompting consideration of new avenues of thought, promoting their self-analysis, setting challenging but realistic targets. This supports the learner's self-esteem by recognising skills and capacities. Research evidence shows that recipients of feedback are less likely to make effective progress if feedback is either too critical and judgemental without appropriate support, or favourable and positive but without an element of challenge. Progress is much more likely if feedback is balanced and shaped to the needs of the recipient.

Giving constructive feedback

All feedback will be, to some extent, subjective. When mentors give feedback, they are offering information, judgement or opinion about an aspect of your performance which s/he may then use to make future changes to that performance. Of course, we hope that when the mentor offers feedback it will be well received and constructively used. While the mentor cannot control how it is received, s/he can take responsibility for how it is offered, and ensure that when they give feedback they do so in a way that is most likely to provide trainees with useful information while valuing them and their achievements to date.

Lesson observation feedback

A possible format is provided below.

Person	Focus	Action
Mentor	General open question	Start by finding out how the trainee feels about the lesson.
Trainee	Strengths	Encourage the trainee to talk about the strengths of the lesson.
Mentor	Strengths	Add your perceptions of these and/or other strengths.
Trainee	Other possibilities	Ask the trainee to identify if aspects could have been different and to look at possible ways that this could be done.
Mentor	Improvements	Raise and discuss other aspects of the teaching which you feel could have been changed.
Mentor and trainee	Targets for the future	Agree targets for the future.

Feedback is most useful and most likely to be heard when it achieves the following.

- **Gives appropriate emphasis to the positive.**
  Most people need encouragement and to be told when they are doing something well. When offering feedback it can really help the recipient to hear what you liked or what you believe they have done well.
  We often tend to emphasise the negative. The focus is likely to be on mistakes more often than strengths. In a rush to criticise, you may overlook the things you liked. If the positive is registered appropriately, any negative is more likely to be listened to, and acted upon.
- **Avoids use of the word 'but'.**
  This tends to negate the previous comment, however positive, and it is often a signal to expect the worst. The word 'and' is a useful alternative that can usually be substituted.
- **Gives specific information about what has been done well.**
  The more specific the information, the more likely it is to be useful. For example, if you know what is being praised, you can build upon that aspect of your work.
- **Gives clear and specific information about what is needed to improve.**
  Again, it is difficult to improve without knowing exactly what needs to be done. This information is important, e.g. it tells you what it was that prevented you from being awarded a higher grade (in the case of formal numerical assessments) and gives you some ways forward for the future.

- **Refers to the learning outcomes and assessment criteria.**
  One of the purposes for providing you with the learning outcomes of a course or module and the criteria by which a particular piece of work will be assessed is to open up the whole process of assessment. You will be encouraged to use the stated outcomes and criteria to guide their work if they are given feedback which relates to those outcomes and criteria.
- **Refers to things that can be changed.**
  It is not likely to be helpful to give a person feedback about something over which they have no choice. Targets should be suggested that are specific, achievable and within a reasonable time limit.
- **Offers alternatives/leaves a choice.**
  If your mentor offers negative feedback, then they should not simply criticise, but suggest what you could have done differently. Turn the negative into a positive suggestion.
  Feedback which demands change may prompt resistance and it appears inconsistent with a belief in each of us being autonomous. It does not involve telling the trainee how they must be to suit you. Skilled feedback offers trainees information about themselves in a way which leaves them with a choice about whether to act on it or not.
- **Is 'owned' by the giver.**
  It is easy for a mentor to say to you *you are . . .*, suggesting that s/he is offering a universally agreed opinion about you. It is important that the mentor takes responsibility for the feedback they offer. Beginning the feedback with 'I' or 'in my opinion' is a way of avoiding the impression of being the giver of 'cosmic judgements' about you.

Receiving and using feedback

Tutors also work with trainees on receiving and using feedback. Just as we selectively perceive what happens in the world around us, so we also selectively hear the information that is fed back to us in the form of feedback. This selection will be based on a number of things, including:

- our own individual judgements about our performance;
- our previous experiences of receiving feedback;
- our beliefs about ourselves and our capability;
- our self-esteem;
- our ability to separate judgements about what we do from judgements about who we are;
- the value we place on the feedback being given;
- the esteem in which we hold the person giving the feedback.

You are encouraged to help yourself by:

- listening to the feedback rather than immediately rejecting or arguing with it;
- being clear about what is being said through requesting clarification from the giver and avoiding the temptation to jump to conclusions;
- asking for feedback in relation to a topic or aspect if it has not been offered.

If you are graded 1–3 then great! But what if you get a 4? Do not despair! Most trainees inevitably get a low grade during their initial observations. Think of this in a positive way, a learning curve, and an opportunity to improve.

CASE STUDY
Here is what Andrew had to say on this issue:
I thought I was doing OK so I was a bit shocked when I was grade a 4. I looked again at the LLUK standards and the Ofsted criteria and I soon realised that my mentor had been very fair and just in his decision. My targets for improvement were numerous but very clearly expressed and they were backed up by a detailed written narrative and a face-to-face meeting. I created a plan from the targets and more important I allowed myself time to reflect on them. Kolb again! My next observations showed that I had distinctly improved and I finally ended up with an overall grade 1.

As Cunningham (2005, p57) says:

> *Experiential learning is probably the one single theoretical perspective likely to be of special utility to mentors. The term is perhaps most frequently associated with the work of Kolb (1984), although there are a number of other writers who examine the key dimensions of learning from experience...coping with challenges, managing learning and preparing to teach can all be enhanced by mentors' skills in facilitating experiential learning.*

Don't forget that your supervising/visiting tutor will also be working closely with your mentor in order to create a balanced and informed account of your progress. During the early part of your training there will be an occasion when your mentor will be accompanied by your tutor, who will benchmark the observation process. This ensures the quality of the process and therefore is of great use to you and your mentor. S/he will be looking at how you are demonstrating your subject-specific expertise and will measure this against Domain C standards. Your tutor's presence in the benchmarking process helps reassure your mentor in the observation procedure.

PRACTICAL TASK PRACTICAL TASK PRACTICAL TASK PRACTICAL TASK PRACTICAL TASK

Once you have completed your second observation by your mentor try to document the processes you followed in order to show that you had developed since your first observation, i.e. feedback–evaluation–preparation and planning–research and discussion. Bullet-point the key features and develop a strategic plan for further development and improvement as you head towards your final two observations.

Triangulation

Finally, as part of your placement experience you should be prepared for the interim and summative triangulation visit (see Chapter 9 for a full discussion on this topic). This is your opportunity to take part in professional discussions and to produce evidence to back up your responses based on your observations, on your teaching file and on your articulation and appropriation of theory to practice. It is a triadic process involving you, your supervising/visiting tutor and your mentor. Examples of how the triangulation meeting may be documented can be found in Chapter 9.

In most providers, triangulation meetings take place half-way through the training (interim) and toward the end (summative). Here is a suggested overview of the practical and professional purposes of the triangulation meetings:

The triangulation document contains details of the subject and groups taught by the trainee; it records achievements and targets against the LLUK standards; and it records an overall holistic grade based upon the criteria specified in the document *Grading Initial Teacher Training 2008–2011* (Ofsted, January 2009). An interim triangulation meeting is held at a mid-point in the professional placement, which is usually the end of February/early March for full-time trainees and May for the part-time trainees. A summative triangulation meeting takes place at the end of the professional placement which is the end of April/early May for the full-time and May for the part-time trainees.

Done well, the interim triangulation can help trainees to focus on areas for further development and enable them to make their teaching and their own students' learning even better. The summative triangulation provides a summative judgement on the trainees' achievements, and indicates further areas for development in their first year of teaching. These can be addressed as part of their continuous professional development, and contribute to the 30-hour CPD, an integral requirement in maintaining their licence to practice.

REFLECTIVE TASK

Once you have had your interim triangulation meeting, document and reflect carefully on how you will use the targets, advice and guidance to improve your potential and aim for a grade 1 in your summative meeting.

I hope you have found this chapter useful in establishing what you should expect from the mentoring experience in your professional placement.

A SUMMARY OF **KEY POINTS**

In this chapter we have considered:

> **what to expect in the initial shadowing period of your placement;**

> **how to prepare for weekly discussions;**

> **the importance of careful planning for observations including evaluation and development;**

> **the process and relevance of triangulation.**

REFERENCES REFERENCES REFERENCES REFERENCES REFERENCES REFERENCES

Cunningham, B (2005) *Mentoring Teachers in Post-compulsory Education.* London: David Fulton.
www.lluk.org/documents/professional_standards_for_itts020107pdf

FURTHER READING FURTHER READING FURTHER READING FURTHER READING

Anthony Coles ed. (2004) *Teaching in Post-Compulsory Education*. David Fulton

Crawley, J (2008) *In at the Deep End: A Survival Guide for Teachers in Post-Compulsory Education*. London: David Fulton.

Bryan Cunningham (2005) *Mentoring Teachers in Post-Compulsory Education*. David Fulton

Garvey, R and Stokes, P and Megginson, D (2009) *Coaching and Mentoring Theory and Practice*. London: Sage.

These are really good books aimed at teachers and mentors in PCET and they can provide you with considerable insight into how special your mentor is in terms of their specific role and their importance in helping you achieve your qualification and give you eligibility for QTLS.

Websites

LLUK
www.lluk.org
Ofsted
www.ofsted.gov.uk

6
Managing behaviour

The objectives of this chapter

This chapter is designed to provide you with some guidance on how to manage the behaviour of your learners and how to have a teaching environment conducive to learning. As a teacher it is important that you model consistent, confident and firm behaviour while allowing students to flourish and explore their own learning. There are practical strategies that can be used in the classroom and hints and tips to enable you to fully develop and to control your environment.

It addresses the following professional practice standards for QTLS:

BK 1.1 Ways to maintain a learning environment in which learners feel safe and supported.

BK 1.2 Ways to develop and manage behaviours which promote respect for and between others and create an equitable and inclusive learning environment.

BK 1.3 Ways of creating a motivating learning environment.

Introduction

The wise teacher uses discretion, represents stability, demonstrates endurance and maintains flexibility. The teacher who would expect certain behaviours of their students can expect cooperation only if those behaviours are important enough for the teacher to meet.

Adapted from Nagel, G (1998, p87) *The Tao of Teaching*

We can see from the press and other media that the post-compulsory education and training sector is rapidly changing and this must be reflected in how we manage the behaviour of learners. To meet the needs of the widely different cohorts, we must ensure we take into account changes in teaching and learning that will be needed to engage 14–16 year old learners as well as those over the age of 16. We should also consider the effect these may have on the behaviour we observe in the classroom and the strategies we employ to ensure learning is taking place.

Behaviour for learning

'Behaviour for learning' is not a traditional concept but it refers to a movement to change in the emphasis from managing 'bad' behaviour to planning for good behaviour. This, for many, is a new way of thinking about behaviour and recognises the key role of lecturers in improving behaviour and in taking responsibility for their role in incidents of challenging behaviour that occur in their classrooms.

It emphasises the crucial link between the way in which young people learn and their social knowledge and behaviour. In doing this the focus is upon establishing positive relationships between staff, students and others.

Young people coming into FE have often had a negative experience in school and FE has a valuable role to play as the sector of the second chance, providing an opportunity for learners to re-engage with learning and to develop their confidence, whether after a long absence or following a negative experience of school. As a result of research and experience it is believed that behaviour for learning can be split into three components: planning, engaging learners and rewarding success.

Planning

Detailed planning will enable you to be proactive rather than reactive in establishing a suitable environment for learning. If you do not give the impression of competence, knowledge and the ability to control and direct learning, then the learners will switch off very quickly and will show their frustration by behaving badly.

Planning sessions to avoid situations that might trigger challenging behaviour and thinking about possible triggers in advance will avoid the opportunities for behaviour to deteriorate, but it is also about planning for and expecting good behaviour. In order to behave well, learners need to be very clear what the ground rules are and what the consequences of breaking the rules will be. It is important that you involve learners in drawing up ground rules and in signing up to those rules, and that you consistently apply those consequences. This means you should experience less disruption and challenging behaviour as learners will be aware of the rules and will see that they are being implemented fairly.

The quality of your lesson planning will have a direct effect on the behaviour in your classroom, therefore planning and organising groups for group work activities beforehand and having this already on the desks or on the board gives learners the impression that it is not negotiable and they have time to adjust to the planned activity.

Being aware of the underlying tensions and issues in a class and subtly reflecting this in the planning ensures that learning can take place and signals to the learners that the lecturer is aware of and listening to their concerns and adapts their planning to reflect this.

You need to reflect regularly on your experiences in the classroom and adapt your strategies accordingly. In reflecting on experiences of challenging behaviour in the classroom it is important to acknowledge the extent of your own responsibilities and the extent to which your actions have influenced the behaviour of the learners. By acknowledging your own role in the incident you can devise strategies for responding differently in the future. Being perceptive to the dynamics of the class and the internal relationships that exist will help you to avoid situations where challenging behaviour can become an issue.

Engaging learners

Young people experience a barrier to learning when something else occupies their minds, preventing them from focusing the necessary attention on what is to be learnt. There are many different things that can cause young people to get distracted or disengaged from learning and it is your job to manage the learning experience but it is difficult to manage any situation unless you take accurate notice of what is happening with your learners and the dynamics in the classroom.

Lessons need to be well structured and planned to engage learners in the learning, activities should be interesting, varied and valuable and the objectives for each activity should be shared with the learners. Learners are less likely to misbehave if they are engaged and working hard and behaviour for learning encourages you to take time and effort in the planning of interesting sessions that are enjoyable and that ensure learning is taking place.

Lecturers are also responsible for ensuring equality and fairness in the classroom. *All students must feel that they are positively and equally valued and accepted, and that their efforts to learn are recognised, and judged without bias* (Petty, 2004, p81).

The second key factor in behaviour for learning is to make sure students are always engaged in their learning and that work is neither to easy nor too difficult. Differentiation is essential to ensure that the needs of all learners are planned for and work is suitable for all learners. *Differentiation is adopting strategies that ensure success in learning for all, by accommo-dating individual differences of any kind* (Petty, 2004, p541).

Learners in FE are very diverse, therefore using a wide range of resources will engage and motivate them and meet the range of their needs. There are many differences between learners that affect their learning. Differentiation is about coping with these differences and using them to promote learning. Differentiated learning takes into account that your learners may differ in terms of their motivation, prior experience and knowledge, learning support needs, cultural expectations, literacy, language, numeracy and ICT levels and their learning preferences. It is important to develop resources that cover more than one level of difficulty, use different media or give your learners choices of how to complete tasks and provide learning support where necessary.

Differentiation enables all learners to participate in learning and reduces the chance of challenging behaviour occurring. This personalisation of learning is very important and ensures that learners feel valued and supported. Working in the FE sector requires a commit-ment from lecturers to adopt an ethos where every learner matters and every learner's learning needs are accommodated as far as is practical and possible.

Rewarding success

One of the most useful ways of encouraging good behaviour is to reward good behaviour and encourage and reward achievement.

Each learner must be respected and valued for who and what she is and a relationship of trust must be built between you and the learner. This is expressed by Rogers (1983) as 'unconditional positive regard'. The lecturer must demonstrate unconditional positive regard for each learner and this will dispose the learner to feel safe and valued, and will improve behaviour. If you are rewarding the learner with trust and respect by using praise to reinforce good behaviour then the learner is unlikely to want to break that trust by behaving badly.

A number of learners in FE have very low self-esteem so by giving out nuggets of praise when it is warranted we can enhance their feelings of self-worth and competence by acknowledging their good qualities and strengths.

CASE STUDY
Tony teaching carpentry and joinery
A trainee lecturer described the following situation that occurred recently in his workshop. A young learner was trying to make a lock, he became frustrated and

disruptive and when challenged by the lecturer he became aggressive, the lecturer responded and the learner 'came at him' with fists raised. The learner was excluded from college and will not return to education. When talking about this the lecturer was adamant that he could have done nothing differently, the boy was violent and had to be disciplined. When questioned further he said *of course I think it started because he could not make the lock*. He then reflected further and said *I suppose I could have helped him or given him an easier task and then it might not have happened*.

The tragic thing about this situation is it could have been avoided by differentiated planning or more personalised activities, but the outcome can't be changed after the event. The learner remains excluded and will probably never return to learning again. The lecturer's response to this reflection was to reluctantly acknowledge some responsibility in the trigger for the situation but to insist that his actions after that point were justified. However, even the reluctant acceptance of responsibility means that he may be more aware and may plan a variety of activities in the future.

REFLECTIVE TASK

1. Discuss this situation with your mentor or a colleague – what do you think could have been done differently?
2. Identify any situations that have happened in your experience and identify the trigger that sparked the incident – consider what action could have been taken to avoid the situation.

CASE STUDY

Dave teaching brickwork

Another trainee talked about his experience of a difficult learner. The learner was constantly disruptive, swearing and distracting other learners. He was quickly disciplined and removed from the course. However, the learner had ADHD and this was acknowledged but no support was put in place. The lecturer said *there is no way I can cope with lads like him when I've got 20 others to manage – he should never have been put in my class*.

In discussion the lecturer admitted that he had always known about the learner's condition, but it was not his job to sort out support.

On further reflection he admitted that he could have chased up support and that if that had been in place the learner might not have been so disruptive. He acknowledged that by planning for that support and adapting his resources the learner could have achieved a positive outcome.

REFLECTIVE TASK

1. Would you have acted differently in this situation? Why?
2. Can you identify people in your organisation that are in a similar situation? What suggestions could you offer them to help them in future?

CASE STUDY

My own experience of teaching travel and tourism

A few years ago I had a learner who was exceptionally disruptive in a non-aggressive way. He was always playing the fool and craving attention. At the time I was convinced I tried everything possible to make him behave, I set up contracts, phoned his parents, had him into my office and told him off, I gave him many chances to improve but nothing worked so I kicked him off the course. Since this point I have found out that he was struggling with his sexuality at the time and was very conflicted in himself. I am ashamed to say I never asked him if there was anything bothering him or offered him any support. I had no inclination of his issues and made no effort to find out.

On reflection, if I hadn't been trying so hard to 'manage' his behaviour I might have been able to see his distress and to offer him emotional support. This might have cured the challenging behaviour.

REFLECTIVE TASK

REFLECTIVE TASK

1. How would 'behaviour for learning' techniques have helped in this situation?
2. Reflect on your own practice and consider any situations in which you could use emotional intelligence in order to control behaviour and ensure your teaching environment is conducive to learning.

The similarities between these three situations are astonishing: all three learners left education and felt let down by the experience, all three situations could have been avoided by the staff utilising behaviour for learning strategies and by being more emotionally intelligent. The college procedures were adhered to in all cases and the bad behaviour was managed, but the learners were not served well by the institution.

Under the new professional standards for teachers, tutors and trainers in the Lifelong Learning Sector the aim of the lecturer is to create a safe learning environment that promotes tolerance, respect and co-operation between learners and lecturers. By using behaviour for learning strategies the classroom will be an environment in which learners are able to participate, voice their opinions, ask questions and be actively involved in how they will learn. By demonstrating emotional intelligence and fostering unconditional positive regard for all learners, students will feel valued as individuals and will be more likely to be engaged and behave in a positive way.

As with most situations in teaching, there is no correct solution to behaviour issues. The important thing is for lecturers to plan for positive behaviour, avoid triggers for bad behaviour and to recognise and avoid the wrong solutions. These wrong solutions will undermine the learner's confidence or motivation, will make matters worse or will put the lecturer in an impossible predicament.

Choosing the course of action to take should be based on careful reflection and consideration of our professional values and not be simply a reactive response.

Emotional intelligence

All lecturers need to develop emotional intelligence and be able to empathise and understand the triggers that cause challenging behaviour.

Daniel Goleman defines emotional intelligence as our ability to be able to motivate ourselves, persist in the face of frustrations, control impulses, to regulate our moods and keep distress from swamping our ability to think, to empathise with others and to hope. (Goleman, 1996).

The fact that we have the ability to control these emotions does not mean that we always do and it takes time and practice to become emotionally intelligent and to use those skills in understanding our learners.

The main use of emotional intelligence in the classroom is in our ability to empathise with others and to put ourselves in their shoes. Young people are going through many changes emotionally and physically, as we will discuss later in this chapter, and it is essential that we try to understand the emotional background to each incident that occurs in our classrooms.

Being able to read body language is another essential tool that allows the lecturer to anticipate and respond quickly to tensions and issues as they arise in the classroom.

It is also our responsibility to develop the emotional intelligence of our students in order for them to be able to understand themselves and empathise with others. Emotional intelligence is our ability to control and use our emotions to enhance our success in all areas of our lives, but in particular in our journey to become lifelong learners.

Much has been written about emotional intelligence and the links to multiple intelligences and studying the work of Howard Gardner and Daniel Goleman would enable you to focus in more depth on this area.

No one learns without using their emotions and those students who behave in a challenging way are often displaying negative emotions in response to previous learning experiences. In order to engage these students we needs to engage their emotions in a positive way during their learning. They need to be enjoying learning and having fun while experiencing unconditional positive regard and receiving praise when it is warranted. By focusing on their positive emotional response you will be minimising their negative emotions and setting them up for a more positive attitude in the future.

To involve learners in emotional learning we need to engage all of their senses in the learning process, we must encourage them to see, hear, feel and be part of the learning process. By immersing themselves in the process of learning they will by default learn what it is we want them to learn.

CASE STUDY

George – training to teach carpentry and joinery

At the start of my Cert Ed course I was dubious as I saw it as 'playing with games' in the classroom with students; I only thought it would be beneficial to pre-school children and not the kind of learner that I teach. These young lads often from a harsh background would think it silly, and I was right; it is silly but not in the way I thought it would be 'pathetic'. I was so wrong that these young lads would not get anything out of the lesson and regret not implementing these valuable resources sooner. Sue Cowley says *Students do respond very well to resources in general, and especially those that are out of the ordinary. The more resources you can bring into your classroom to use, the more you will find the behaviour of your students improving* (Cowley, 2007. p107).

Since 'seeing the light' I have implemented several creative resources. I must admit that most of them are borrowed ideas from other people within the education sector, but adapted to suit the needs of carpentry and joinery. The change in the attitude of the learners is quite remarkable. To see these particular students with 'street cred' to uphold, really enjoying cutting up lollipops sticks and sticking them together to make models is an amazing experience. These students are more emotionally involved in the sessions and are much better behaved.

PRACTICAL TASK PRACTICAL TASK **PRACTICAL TASK** PRACTICAL TASK **PRACTICAL TASK**

1. Take some time to think about your resources – what else could you use to vary your sessions?
2. Take one of these ideas and implement it in the classroom – does it work? Is behaviour better?

How students learn

When we 'learn' in ordinary situations (with a book or a teacher), we are actually using less than 20 per cent of our brain's capacity. Our learning potential isn't fixed. Intelligence is a group of abilities that can be developed.

Accelerated learning is one technique that encourages us to maximise the learning opportunities for our learners by thinking about how they learn and using this information in the planning of our sessions. Accelerated learning, also known as 'super-learning' or 'brain-friendly learning', is a system designed to help people of all ages learn more and retain more by using the whole of the brain.

Left- and right-brain thinking

Traditional methods of learning concentrate on the left side of the brain (which controls our powers of language, logic and sequencing) more than the right side (which deals with forms and patterns, rhythm, space and imagination). Creating connections between both sides when we learn stimulates electrical–chemical impulses so that our 100 billion active brain cells work harder.

We can learn many things simultaneously, like the tune, rhythm and words to a song. This demonstrates that learning is not confined to one part of the brain, but can happen in both parts at once.

Learning by doing

Since we learn to talk by talking, swim by swimming and drive by driving, it makes sense to make learning anything as practical and activity-based as possible. Working collaboratively (in a group) is ideal, because a learning 'community' will have more success than a collection of isolated individuals.

Accelerated learning increases your ability to learn by stimulating your brain to work harder. This can be done by creating new practical learning situations such as using drama to learn about science. If it's done as a group activity, the experience can be fun and rewarding.

For instance, students could build a giant floor model of a complex chemical compound, or create a one-minute drama about the life cycle of an insect or a key moment in history. Instead of simply writing about it, students might write a rap song about a complex geographical process.

The experiences will be memorable, so more will be learnt – and that will increase the desire for more learning.

Reviewing learning

Another important aspect of accelerated learning methods is to review new knowledge during the learning process. Studies show that the human brain forgets much of the information it processes during one day if that information isn't reviewed.

To help your students remember what they have learnt, encourage them to talk about the main points each day. At the end of each week, get your class to review the main points again. They will be a step ahead when they come to revise for exams or assessments, too.

Boys v girls

It is also important to note that research has shown that boys and girls have slightly different brains and learn best in different ways. Girls seem to be more emotionally and socially grounded within this age range, seemingly making it easier for them to cope with situations of intense academic pressure and transition.

Behavioural expectations among peer groups are more demanding for boys. Clever boys may find themselves under more pressure than girls to behave to the detriment of their learning.

Girls are more able to plan and organise themselves in order to complete coursework than boys. Most assessment methods using coursework disadvantage boys who would have traditionally achieved well in exams.

Boys tend to seek assistance only as a last resort, whereas girls will ask for guidance and support throughout their learning.

Lots of the activities we use in the classroom are 'girl friendly' and we need to consider activities like brain gym, competition and the use of ICT to ensure boys are engaged as well.

Having a choice of assessment methods or activities may allow both boys and girls to achieve equally in your classroom.

Following the procedures that exist in your organisation

It is essential that you find out the procedures that exist in your organisation for dealing with challenging behaviour.

It is likely there will be a system of warnings that take place before formal discipline procedures are implemented. You also need to be clear about the levels of behaviour that relate to each stage.

Certain serious behaviours will result in immediate discipline procedures such as suspension and you need to be clear what you should do in these situations. These types of behaviours normally involve violence towards yourself or other students, drug abuse and serious damage to property or theft. These will not be within your control and you should immediately refer them to the appropriate person.

Where behaviour is merely 'challenging' (swearing, not working, not doing homework, talking throughout the lesson, not being prepared and not handing in work) you need to make your own decision as to when they are serious enough to warrant a warning.

An example of this might be if a student swears 'accidentally' in the heat of a discussion. You may decide that it is not worth a warning but you may have a quiet word at the end of the class explaining why it is not appropriate. However, where a student uses bad language in an aggressive way you may feel a warning is appropriate straight away.

You need to be very clear about what is and is not acceptable in your classroom and your organisation and then you need to apply those rules consistently.

If you are going to give a student a warning it is important to explain to them in person exactly why you are doing it and what improvements you expect in the future. If you let it come as a surprise to the student they will be more likely to hold a grudge and to continue to behave in a challenging way in your class.

Dealing with challenging behaviour

As we have mentioned previously in this chapter, you need to set your ground rules at the start and revisit them regularly. If you experience challenging behaviour you need to have some strategies in place to deal with it. First of all remember it is your classroom and you decide what is and is not acceptable.

Consider using some of the following.

- Approach the student involved and, getting down to their level, quietly explain to them that the behaviour is unacceptable and you are giving them the chance to improve their behaviour.
- Stand slightly behind the student in question and continue to teach the lesson.
- Use positive language such as *thank you for stopping talking to listen to this important information*.
- Never say please but always say thank you. Saying *please will you be quiet* gives them a choice in their actions. Saying *thank you for being quiet* assumes they are going to follow your instruction.
- Give disruptive students a role. Ask them to write something on the whiteboard or hand out some papers. This gives them a break from their behaviour and allows them to calm down.

- Never get into a face-to-face confrontation with a student. Always keeps them after the class and talk quietly and calmly about how you want them to change their behaviour.
- Never make threats unless you are able to carry them out. However, do have consequences ready. For example: *if we are able to finish this part of the lesson quietly in the next ten minutes you can have a break, if not there will not be time*.
- Remember to use praise to encourage good behaviour.
- Be confident enough to allow some deviation from your lesson if it is allowing discussion and learning is taking place. A quiet classroom does not always mean learning is taking place.
- Try to remember that the amount of time and effort you have put into your planning does not mean they will automatically enjoy the lesson. Sometimes our own frustration makes us react to them and things get blown out of all proportion. For example: If someone says an activity is boring and it has taken you three hours of preparation including laminating, you are more likely to react badly. Try saying *I am sorry you are finding it boring. How could I change it in the future to ensure you find it interesting? Please write down your suggestions and I will talk to you about them at the end*. This may ensure they don't tell you they are bored again but you might also get some valuable suggestions.
- Always follow through by having a chat with students outside of the class. Ask for their thoughts about the lesson and why they felt the need to behave inappropriately. Listen to what they say and be prepared to learn something yourself. It is not just about 'telling them off' but about understanding their behaviour and avoiding it in the future.
- If you are unsure about dealing with a situation, always ask your mentor or a colleague for advice and get someone to sit with you when you talk to the student if it helps.
- Remember that although in 80 per cent of cases challenging behaviour can be avoided or dealt with easily sometimes students are just naughty. Try to isolate these occasions and deal firmly with them.
- You will not get it right all of the time so give yourself a break – don't beat yourself up about incidences where you have got it wrong, just reflect on them and do it differently next time.

CASE STUDY

Dawn – training to teach counselling

When you encounter teaching for the first time you can be overwhelmed by the need to want your learners to achieve. Throughout your training you are being constantly reminded that your sessions should be well structured, innovative, incorporate learning style, use all available resources plus more essentially have fun. Therefore you tend to find your bag is full of everything ranging from Post-it notes to sweets, all in the hope it will motivate and enable your learners to achieve.

Therefore arriving at a session to find half of the learners unaccounted for and the ones that have turned up are in the middle of raging World War Three on each other can for you as the teacher be very daunting. This for me was exactly what I did encounter during one of my first teaching sessions.

It was through this first experience that it has become apparent to me that learners need to be self-motivated enough to come into the classroom in the first place. Whatever their age, learning style or the level of the course they need to be motivated by us to want to turn up again and to be willing to learn in each session.

I recognise that all of our educational experiences are different and this can have either a positive or a negative influence upon our future learning.

If you as a teacher are motivated I believe your learners will be just as much. Struggling with poor motivation in students can be really difficult as one unhappy 16-year-old can soon turn 20 of them.

Promising learners the world will not encourage or motivate them, but the correct encouragement and support aids the learners to want to learn more. This is evident on the course on which I teach. The learners feed off positive motivation and want to learn more. This is when ownership for their own learning must take place and is reflected through their own results and achievements.

It must be recognised that lack of motivation and challenging behaviour cannot be stamped out entirely but through working with learners on a more personal level I have found that within a college environment this has had very positive effects and is worth my time and effort in planning and facilitating this type of learning environment.

REFLECTIVE TASK

1. What would you do in Dawn's situation with the class waging war?
2. Have you ever dealt with a situation like this? What would you do differently next time?

15 'top tips' for a well-behaved classroom

1. Take time with the planning – plan interesting and varied lessons with lots of practical activities to avoid students getting bored.
2. Set ground rules – revisit them regularly so no one can forget.
3. Be consistent – challenge rule-breaking on every occasion.
4. Be fair – treat all students equally and fairly at all times, do not play favourites.
5. Follow through – never threaten something you are not going to (or are not able to) follow through.
6. Think before you react – try to identify the trigger and deal with that, not the resulting behaviour.
7. Use praise thoughtfully and meaningfully – whenever it is earned.
8. Use humour – don't be afraid to laugh at your self.
9. Get to know your students – understand their journeys and personalities.
10. Be friendly but firm – don't show weakness or uncertainty.
11. Ask for feedback – and don't be afraid to act on their suggestions.
12. Say what you mean and mean what you say – make sure instructions are clear and repeated.
13. Use positive body language – be aware of the students' body language.
14. Deal with challenging behaviour outside of the classroom – don't tell students off in front of their peers.
15. Finally, be pleasant, polite and efficient and you won't go far wrong.

A SUMMARY OF **KEY POINTS**

In this chapter we have:

> explored the concept of behaviour for learning;

> discussed the role of emotional intelligence in managing behaviour;

> considered the issues around how students learn;

> identified strategies that can be used in managing challenging behaviour.

REFERENCES REFERENCES REFERENCES **REFERENCES** REFERENCES REFERENCES

Cowley, S (2006) *Getting the Buggers to Behave.* London: Continuum.
Goleman, D (2005) *Emotional Intelligence.* London: Bantam Books.
Petty, G (2004) *Teaching Today.* Cheltenham: Nelson Thornes.

FURTHER READING FURTHER READING **FURTHER READING** FURTHER READING

Cowley, S (2006) *Getting the Buggers to Behave.* London: Continuum.
Dix, P (2007) *Taking Care of Behaviour.* Harlow: Pearson.
Steward, A (2008) *Getting the Buggers to Learn in FE.* London: Continuum.
Dave Vizard (2007) *How to Manage Behaviour in Further Education.* Paul Chapman Publishing
    This book is a very good, clearly written text that gives very clear and simple advice and guidance on managing behaviour. It focuses particularly on 14–19 year olds and provides some practical examples of resources to use on the CD included.
Susan Wallace (2007) *Managing Behaviour in the Lifelong Learning Sector.* Learning Matters
    This book is good because it focuses on specific issues that occur in the Lifelong Learning Sector and is full of useful hints and tips. This is particularly useful for people new to teaching.

Websites

Dave Vizard's Behaviour Solutions
    www.behaviourmatters.com
Teaching Ideas
    www.teachingideas.co.uk
Teachers TV
    www.teachers.tv

7
Structure and organisation

The objectives of this chapter

This chapter is intended to help you recognise those interested parties who will influence what and how you teach.

By the end of this chapter you should be able to recognise the drivers and levers within the sector that shape your planning in terms of content and your students' learning in terms of assessment. From a career point of view, being informed as to the broader agenda for the sector and being aware of its major stakeholders will ensure that your work is relevant and contemporary.

It also addresses the following professional standards for QTLS:

AK 2.2 Ways in which learning promotes the emotional, intellectual, social and economic well-being of individuals and the population as a whole.

AK 6.1 Relevant statutory requirements and codes of practice.

CK 1.2 Ways in which own specialism relates to the wider social, economic and environmental context.

EK 5.3 The necessary/appropriate assessment information to communicate to others who have a legitimate interest in learner achievement.

Introduction – a sector of constant change

Dame Ruth Silver, quoted by Thomson (2009), in her valedictory interview with the TES (**www.tes.co.uk**) concludes, *basically, if you want a world that doesn't change then don't work in FE*.

It is necessary to recognise what is behind that remark to understand the significance for a new teacher and the possible impact on their work.

PRACTICAL TASK PRACTICAL TASK PRACTICAL TASK PRACTICAL TASK PRACTICAL TASK

1. Make a list of five changes that you know have taken place in the post-compulsory sector in the last five years.
2. For each item in the list, write a statement noting how it has affected, or how you think it might affect your work in the classroom or workshop.

If you have found it hard to identify five changes, read the section below carefully and make use of the references provided to find out more. A useful tip is to look for summaries of the reports which are often produced by government departments or by other interested parties, such as awarding bodies, to disseminate the key points more effectively.

Obviously, across any timescale change will be apparent, but it is the regularity of significant change across the post-compulsory sector, affecting organisations and individuals involved in planning, management and delivery, that is important and which has impact right down to the individual teacher.

For example, even the name of the sector is changeable. In the last 20 years the sector, or some component parts, has been known by names such as 'Further Education', 'Tertiary Education', 'Adult and Community Education', 'Learning and Skills', 'Lifelong Learning', 'Work-based Learning' and 'Post-compulsory Education and Training'. It could be argued that this inconsistency in name reflects an uncertainty over the focus of the sector and its agencies.

However, the consequence of change is that the professionally engaged QTLS teacher will need to respond to and, in some cases, anticipate the way in which vision and policy translate into practice in the classroom or workshop.

Government change – structure, policy, implementation

The sector is also a victim of government change. In 2007 the Department for Education and Skills (DfES) was split into the Department for Children, Families and Schools (DCFS) and the Department for Innovation, Universities and Skills (DIUS). But these were merely the latest incarnations: DfES was formerly the Department for Education and Employment, 1995–2001, which had been the Department for Education, 1992–1995, and in turn the Department for Education and Science, 1964–1992. Five government departments in 15 years with the names reflecting the current focus and expectation of the government of the time.

You might think that such change doesn't work its way down to the classroom. However, one clear example of ambiguity can be seen in the tussle between DCFS and DIUS over the 14–19 Curriculum and new diplomas which were found to be straddling both departments of state. And, of course, at the time of writing (summer 2009) we have just seen the demise of DIUS, to be replaced by the Department of Business, Innovation and Skills (BIS).

Changes to the college organisation and curriculum

From the early 1990s onwards the sector saw change to its core identity, its essential curriculum and to its relationship with its learners. There was the 'incorporation' of colleges as a result of the Further and Higher Education Act 1992, moving them out of the control of the local education authority into independent corporation status. This provided greater freedom but also greater risk, as shown by those colleges that were not run efficiently enough to be financially sound and had to close or merge.

New curricula in the form of NVQs, GNVQs and changes to A levels introduced in Curriculum 2000 required different teaching, learning and assessment strategies. Furthermore, there was a series of major reports seeking greater purpose and greater effectiveness in the sector. Dearing (1996) reviewed the whole purpose and effectiveness of qualifications within post-16 education; Tomlinson (1996) and Kennedy (1997) examined the nature of inclusion and the benefits of learning for the wider community; and Moser (1999) challenged the deficiencies in teaching basic skills to adults. The early years of the twenty-first century saw one of the most radical reports – that of Tomlinson (2004), which sought to resolve the conflict between so-called academic and vocation qualifications and which resulted in the new 14–19 diplomas being launched in 2008. By presenting an overarching review of the sector, Foster (2005) asked colleges to engage more closely with their local economic community and to be more responsive to demand. Leitch (2006) laid out the need and the strategy to develop an economically competitive and skilled workforce by 2020. While the recommendations of such reports are never implemented without some government modification, their impact on policy and practice in the sector was, and still is, significant.

Change was happening at each and every key point: it was truly endemic to the sector. The Further Education Funding Council, created by the Further and Higher Education Act 1992 and abolished by the Learning and Skills Act 2000, and the Training and Enterprise Councils, active over the same period, were replaced by the Learning and Skills Council (LSC) to be the driver of a demand-led curriculum and the regulator of funding. (The LSC itself, having operated for less than ten years, is on the cusp of being replaced by the Young People's Learning Agency and the Skills Funding Agency, reporting to DCSF and BIS respectively.) But what has this got to do with teaching in the classroom?

Impact on the classroom

PRACTICAL TASK PRACTICAL TASK PRACTICAL TASK PRACTICAL TASK PRACTICAL TASK

Write down three reasons why a teacher takes a register.

You probably said to monitor attendance; to have a list of those present in the event of a fire; and something about complying with legislation, or needing to keep accurate records.

At the risk of oversimplifying the situation, the register is a key tool in guaranteeing the economic survival of any college or training provider in the sector. Used in conjunction with college administrative systems, a register is a way of ensuring learners are on an appropriate course, that they are actually enrolled on the course, that they undertake assessment and that their results are recorded. Omissions in any part of this process will result in a loss of funding.

While it is not necessary for teachers to fully understand LSC funding regulations, you must appreciate the importance of your part in managing the learner journey from interview, through enrolment, learning, assessment and achievement. Because of discrepancies and errors in the records regarding enrolments colleges can lose tens of thousands of pounds in funding, and that, frankly, translates into lost jobs.

Changes in initial teacher training for the sector

In terms of workforce development, national training organisations (NTOs) have been replaced by Sector Skills Councils across all professional training sectors. Particularly relevant is the change of Further Education National Training Organisation (FENTO) to Lifelong Learning UK (LLUK).

The White Paper *Success for All: Reforming further education* (DfES, 2002) was instrumental in accelerating the change from FENTO teaching and learning standards to the new LLUK Standards (2007), which you will see elsewhere in this text. It was this paper and the review *The Initial Training of Further Education Teachers*, by OfSTED (2003), that led to the development of a new framework of qualifications identified as appropriate for those wishing to teach in the sector.

The DfES published *Equipping our Teachers for the Future: Reforming Initial Teacher Training for the Learning and Skills Sector* in 2004. This policy document saw the FENTO Standards (see Lucas, 2005) for teaching and supporting learning, introduced as recently as 2001, being replaced by the new LLUK Standards in 2007 together with the advent of QTLS. The course that you are now studying will be based on these standards and you will have to complete your course and then undertake and evidence your professional formation in order to achieve QTLS.

Although consultations have been a regular part of these changes , it is clear that there has been a top-down drive to develop content skills and professionalism within ITT for the sector and the impact is evident as you enter both the staff room and the classroom.

Demand, supply and support

This section outlines a range of organisations that seek to determine, to influence or to support the work of the individual teacher in the classroom or workshop.

A description is provided of their function and related roles together with some commentary as to how this might affect your work.

Demand

Department for Children Families and Schools (DCFS) www.dcsf.gov.uk
The Department for Children, Families and Schools (DCFS) lists its aims as wanting to:

- make children and young people happy and healthy;
- keep them safe and sound;
- give them a top class education;
- help them stay on track.

Two key areas are Every Child Matters (ECM) and the Children's Plan. Although the names suggest younger children than we would expect to see in the post-compulsory sector, colleges have had to engage with ECM and ensure aspects are addressed within the curriculum. You may see this renamed as 'Every Learner Matters' in some college literature and you will see it as part of some colleges' session plan templates. Not all colleges have adopted an explicit route to covering ECM so you will need to enquire of your mentor how it is addressed in your placement.

The aim of the Every Child Matters programme is to give all children and young people the support they need to:

- be healthy;
- stay safe;

- enjoy and achieve;
- make a positive contribution;
- achieve economic well-being.

See **www.dcsf.gov.uk/everychildmatters**

The Every Child Matters agenda has been further developed through publication of the Children's Plan in December 2007. The Plan aims to improve educational outcomes, improve health, reduce offending rates among young people and eradicate child poverty by 2020. The are many agencies involved in this strategy and the post-compulsory sector is among them, so awareness of this will be important to your work.

There are also areas of DCFS dealing specifically with 14–19 education, including functional skills, 14–16 re-engagement, 14–19 diplomas and A levels. See **www.dcsf.gov.uk/14-19**

Department for Business, Innovation and Skills (BIS) www.dius.gov.uk
In the Department's own words:

> *Britain can only succeed in a rapidly changing world if we develop the skills of our people to the fullest possible extent, carry out world class research and scholarship, and apply both knowledge and skills to create an innovative and competitive economy.*
>
> *The work of BIS – on further and higher education, innovation, science and technology, intellectual property, and supporting evidence-based policy making across government – is therefore essential to national prosperity.*
>
> **www.dius.gov.uk**

One key area identified is learning and skills. Here the department will take responsibility for all post-19 learning – from basic literacy to postdoctoral work – and will seek to make provision for people at every stage of their adult lives. The link between skills, economic prosperity and personal aspirations is outlined strongly within the Department's remit. They speak of creating an accessible education system to give people the skills they need to prosper and assert that to meet the needs of business the same system must provide people with the skills they need now and in the future.

This focus on accessibility and providing skills to meet the needs of business will translate into an expectation that colleges review and revise their curriculum offer accordingly. One result may be that the subject you entered the sector to teach may not be the same subject you find yourself teaching in ten years' time. But things aren't going to change that much are they?

REFLECTIVE TASK

1. There are a number of YouTube clips of a presentation called *Did you Know?* by Karl Fisch and Scott McLeod.

    Put 'Did You Know 3.0 Fisch McLeod' into a search engine and enjoy five minutes of the revealing pace of change.

2. Consider how these changes might impact on your own teaching or training.

Learning and Skills Council (LSC) www.lsc.gov.uk

The LSC's major tasks have been to:

- raise participation and achievement by young people;
- increase adult demand for learning;
- raise skills levels for national competitiveness;
- improve the quality of education and training delivery;
- equalise opportunities through better access to learning;
- improve the effectiveness and efficiency of the sector.

This was done through planning and funding education and training for everyone in the post-compulsory sector in England, other than those in universities.

Recent legislation has seen the work of the LSC divided between local authorities and two new bodies, the Young People's Learning Agency (YPLA) and the Skills Funding Agency (SFA). (At the time of writing (August 2009) there are no active websites for these bodies.)

The Young People's Learning Agency (YPLA) will form part of the wider 16–19 system, together with local authorities, working in their regions and sub-regions, and government offices. It is intended to be a *new slim-line body, committed to reducing unnecessary bureaucracy*. One of its primary roles will be to support local authorities commissioning learning and skills for 16–19 year olds, with specific responsibilities such as, for example, ensuring that regions and local authorities get the right funding.

The Skills Funding Agency (SFA) will have a principal function of routing funding to FE colleges and other providers, primarily in response to customer (employer and learner) choice on programmes, such as Train to Gain.

It will operate through the following:

- National Apprenticeship Service;
- Employer Skills Services;
- Adult Advancement and Careers Service;
- Learner Skills Services.

It intends to work as a demand-led system that will respond to the need for skills and training emerging from employers and adults, rather than trying to plan supply. In funding terms this means FE colleges and training providers will receive funding as they attract customers (learners or employers), rather than receiving a block grant based upon estimates of expected demand.

The potential impact for teachers in the sector is the need for their teaching and training, particularly in the skills curriculum, to be current, adaptive to skills need and employment patterns, and flexible.

Alliance of Sector Skills Councils (ASSC) www.sscalliance.org.uk

The Alliance is an organisation comprising all 25 licensed UK Sector Skills Councils (SSCs), the employer-driven organisations that articulate the voice of the employers of around 90 per cent of the UK's workforce on skills issues.

Its core purpose is stated to:

- act as the collective voice of the SSCs;
- promote understanding of the role of SSCs within the skills system across England, Scotland, Wales and Northern Ireland;
- co-ordinate policy positions and strategic work on skills with stakeholders across the four home nations;
- help build the performance capability of the SSCs to ensure they continue to work effectively on the employer-driven skills agenda.

Skills for Business www.sectorcareersinfo.co.uk

All 25 Sector Skills Councils which make up the Alliance of SSCs have joined together to establish an information advice and guidance initiative, Skills for Business. The aim of the initiative is to provide accurate information on jobs and skills to careers bodies, individual careers practitioners and those who give informal careers advice.

UK Commission for Employment and Skills (UK CES) www.ukces.org.uk

Established by government in April 2008, the UK Commission for Employment and Skills is a key recommendation in Lord Leitch's 2006 review of skills. The UK Commission was originally created by the merger of two predecessor organisations, the Sector Skills Development Agency and the National Employer Panel.

Regional development

There are also immediate local and regional stakeholders who will seek to engage with colleges. These include, in England, the Regional Development Agencies (RDAs) **www.englandsrdas.com** who are strategic leaders, seeking to develop regional economies by matching workforce to opportunity and with associated involvement in appropriate curriculum. In Scotland this is the responsibility of the Scottish government and in Wales of the Welsh Assembly.

Scottish Government **www.scotland.gov.uk/Topics/Education**
Welsh Assembly **http://wales.gov.uk/topics/educationandskill**

Supply

Lifelong Learning UK (LLUK) www.lluk.org.uk

Lifelong Learning UK (LLUK) is the sector skills council responsible for the professional development of those working in further education, work-based learning, higher education, career guidance, community learning and development, libraries and information services across the UK.

As can be seen by the way in which this book identified the LLUK standards throughout, it is an essential agency in the development of initial teacher training in the sector. While it is necessary to recognise and respect diversity, the role of LLUK, it could be argued, has been to develop an agreed minimum of knowledge and skill to be effective in the sector. How pervasive such a template will become and to what extent all employers will agree with it is not yet decided. You will come across colleagues in your organisation who pre-date both FENTO and LLUK in their training. This does not make them unqualified or poor teachers. It is, however, more likely that you have more of your career ahead of you and so should engage with professional development as fully as possible to maximise your opportunities and your professional satisfaction.

The Qualifications and Curriculum Development Agency (QCDA)
www.qcda.org.co.uk
The Qualifications and Curriculum Development Agency (QCDA) sees itself as being *at the heart of England's education system. Our job will be to develop the curriculum, improve and deliver assessments, and review and reform qualifications*.

The Qualifications and Curriculum Authority (QCA) was set up under the Education Act 1997 to develop and regulate the national curriculum, assessments in schools and qualifications. In 2007 the government decided to set up an independent exams regulator, Ofqual (see below), which has now taken on most of QCA's regulatory functions.

QCDA's stated intention is to:

work with schools and colleges on:

- The curriculum – *we'll listen to what teachers tell us, and together we'll build a curriculum that will prepare young people for the future.*
- Assessment – *as well as delivering the national curriculum tests, we want to develop ways of assessing pupils' progress that support teaching and that are manageable in the classroom.*
- Qualifications – *together we'll review and develop qualifications, so that students have the knowledge and skills they need to take them into higher education and work.*

They also declare they will:

work with businesses on:
- Qualifications that help people get the right skills – *such as the Diploma, which combines classroom and workplace learning.*
- The Qualifications and Credit Framework – *a new system that lets people build up their qualifications in small steps so that all their learning is recognised, including training at work.*

(**www.qcda.org.uk**)

Office of the Qualifications and Examinations Regulator (Ofqual)
www.ofqual.gov.uk
Ofqual, the Office of the Qualifications and Examinations Regulator, is the new regulator of qualifications, tests and examinations in England. Some of their keys aims include:

- ensuring that organisations that offer and deliver qualifications (awarding organisations) have good systems in place, and that they are held to account for their performance;
- ensuring that all qualifications offered by awarding organisations are fair and are comparable with other qualifications;
- ensuring that standards in qualifications, exams and tests are monitored and the findings are reported;
- ensuring that there is fair access to qualifications for all candidates;
- ensuring that the qualifications market provides value for money and meets the needs of learners and employers.

Awarding bodies
The awarding bodies have to respond to the parameters established by QCDA and Ofqual. In practical terms this will be seen in the duration of examinations set for your learners, in the

language used, in the type of assessment strategy, in content and in grading and mark schemes.

Some of the awarding bodies you are most likely to come across include:

- AQA;
- OCR;
- Edexcel;
- NCFE;
- City & Guilds;
- ILM;
- Construction Awards Alliance;
- AAT.

As discussed in Chapter 2, awarding bodies can be the source of essential information and valuable updating events. Enter the name into a search engine and you will find essential resources. Read carefully and ensure you have the current, up-to-date version of all appropriate documents. Look for subject-specific workshops or conferences and apply early.

Office for Standards in Education (Ofsted) www.ofsted.gov.uk/

Ofsted inspects and regulates across the full range from early years to education and skills for learners of all ages. As training and education in the workplace has moved towards more external and nationally recognised qualifications, Ofsted now inspects within the NHS, within prisons and within police forces.

The best way to prepare for an Ofsted inspection is to be confident that you know the criteria on which your teaching will be evaluated and to be familiar with the inspection framework. The criteria and associated grading are available from the Ofsted website although it is likely your course provider has already made them available to you. You should use the Ofsted website to look at reports on similar colleges and providers and at similar subject areas to identify the strengths and the weaknesses and to respond accordingly.

Learning and Skills Improvement Service (LSIS) www.lsis.org.uk

The Learning and Skills Improvement Service (LSIS) came into operation in October 2008. It resulted from the merger of the Centre for Excellence in Leadership (CEL) and the Quality Improvement Agency (QIA).

LSIS is expected to focus on learners and on developing and providing *sustainable further education and skills* across the sector. Leadership development is intended to underpin and form an important part of its role in the sector, being based on the earlier work of CEL.

It is included in the 'supply' category rather than the support category because it has a direct remit to support and develop those areas of the sector that government departments specifically identify as needing to respond better.

Association of Colleges (AoC) www.aoc.co.uk

The Association of Colleges (AoC) is the body that represents and promotes the interests of colleges and provides its members with professional support services. The AoC was established in 1996 by colleges themselves looking to provide a voice for further education and higher education delivered in colleges.

The AoC negotiates with the relevant trade unions to agree pay and conditions. However, not all organisations in the sector are in a sufficiently strong financial position to implement agreed recommendations. One result of this, and an outcome from incorporation, is that there are variations in the interpretation and application of pay and conditions across the sector. Thus the salary for two seemingly similar jobs might be quite different.

Association of Learning Providers (ALP) www.learningproviders.org.uk

The Association of Learning Providers (ALP) is an organisation of work-based training providers that mirrors the AoC for the non-college part of the sector.

Its goal is to influence the education, skills and employment agenda to secure:

- an integrated employment and skills strategy meeting employer and individual needs;
- a 14–19 learning curriculum giving equal weight to the vocational and academic;
- opportunities for lifelong learning and sustainable employment for all;
- a government-supported market open to all providers offering high-quality learning.

Association of Teachers and Lecturers (ATL) www.atl.org.uk

The ATL is an education union that clearly straddles both the compulsory and non-compulsory sectors. It has grown steadily since the 1980s and now supports 160,000 members across the UK.

University and College Union (UCU) www.ucu.org.uk

The University and College Union (UCU) represents more than 120,000 academics, lecturers, trainers, instructors, researchers, in universities, colleges, prisons, adult education and training organisations across the UK.

UCU claims to be the largest post-school union in the world. It was formed on in June 2006 by the amalgamation of the Association of University Teachers (AUT) and NATFHE, the University and College Lecturers' Union, who shared a long history of defending and advancing educators' employment and professional interests.

These unions are the lead negotiators engaged with the employers over pay and conditions for the sector.

Support

Institute for Learning (IfL) www.ifl.ac.uk

The Institute for Learning (IfL) is the professional body for teachers, trainers and assessors across further education (FE), including adult and community learning, emergency and public services, the armed services, the voluntary sector and work-based learning. You must join the IfL to achieve QTLS and must record your annual undertaking of continual professional development to maintain your status.

Learning and Skills Network (LSN) www.lsnlearning.org.uk

The Learning and Skills Network is an independent, not-for-profit agency using research and training to support the development of the sector. Their focus is the development of staff, enhancement of services and improvement of organisations.

Best practice is shared through conferences and training events supplemented by a variety of publications addressing the latest themes and developments in the learning and skills sector.

The virtual and real networks we develop present valuable opportunities for leaders, managers and practitioners to share best practice. These networks always generate new ideas, resources and approaches that can be further disseminated through our events and publications.

Becta www.becta.org.uk/

Becta is the government agency leading the drive to ensure the effective and innovative use of technology throughout learning.

Its stated ambition is *to utilise the benefits of technology to create a more exciting, rewarding and successful experience for learners of all ages and abilities, enabling them to achieve their potential*. It aims to do this by leading the delivery and development of e-strategy, and by seeking to influence the strategic direction and development of national education policy so as to best take advantage of new and emerging technology.

The National Institute of Adult Continuing Education (NIACE) www.niace.org.uk

The National Institute of Adult Continuing Education (NIACE) has an aim of encouraging all adults to engage in learning of all kinds. It seeks to do this by campaigning and lobbying, providing consultancies and supporting practitioners by publishing research, journals and textbooks.

Third Sector National Learning Alliance (TSNLA) www.tsnla.org.uk/

The Third Sector National Learning Alliance (TSNLA) is a an alliance of voluntary and community organisations and social enterprises involved in learning and skills. It aims to provide a 'voice' from and for third sector providers and a forum for developing third sector ideas and proposals. Work on the TSNLA began in 2006 through a partnership between the National Institute of Adult Continuing Education (NIACE) and the UK Workforce Hub.

PRACTICAL TASK PRACTICAL TASK PRACTICAL TASK PRACTICAL TASK PRACTICAL TASK

1. Talk to colleagues, particularly your mentor, about change and development in the sector. Consider what the impact on your teaching might be if you are not up to date with course content, assessment regulations, new initiatives.
2. List three areas or topics about which you think you need more information. Use the links provided to research this.

The continuous rate of change in the sector, driven very publicly by government exhortation to transform the lives of our learners and the skills base of the economy can create frustrations and anxieties. The best coping strategy is to be proactive, to recognise the major interested parties and their agents and to be well informed as to current practice and future policy.

There are many supporting networks – this chapter has identified only a few. Use them, join them, contribute to them.

To engage in this way not only provides a sound basis on which to develop your teaching but it will provide opportunities for career development beyond the classroom or workshop, into areas such as support, publishing, consultancy and leadership.

A SUMMARY OF **KEY POINTS**

In this chapter we have:

> explored the recent changes in PCET and their effect on your practice;

> discussed the role of the different demand, supply and support organisations in the sector;

> considered how these might affect you in your current practice and future career;

> identified agencies that can support you in developing your role.

REFERENCES REFERENCES REFERENCES **REFERENCES** REFERENCES REFERENCES

Dearing, R (1996) *Review of Qualifications for 16–19 Year Olds*. London: HMSO.

DfES (2002) *Success for All. Reforming Further Education*. London: HMSO.

DfES (2004) *Equipping our Teachers for the Future: Reforming Initial Teacher Training for the Learning and Skills Sector*. London: HMSO.

Foster, A (2005) *Realising the Potential. A Review of the Future Role of Further Education Colleges*. London: DfES.

Kennedy, H (1997) *Learning Works*. London: FEFC.

Leitch, S (2006) *Leitch Review of Skills.* London: HMSO.

LLUK (2007) *Guidance for Awarding Institutions on Teacher Roles and Initial Teaching Qualifications*. London: LLUK.

Lucas, N (2004) The 'FENTO Fandango': National Standards, Compulsory Teaching Qualifications and the Growing Regulation of FE College Teachers. *Journal of Further and Higher Education,* 28 (1): 35–51.

Moser, C (1999) *A Fresh Start – Improving Literacy and Numeracy.* London: DfEE.

Ofsted (2003) *The Initial Training of Further Education Teachers*, HMI 1762. London: Ofsted.

Tomlinson, J (1996) *Inclusive Learning*. London: FEFC.

Tomlinson, M (2004) *14–19 Curriculum and Qualifications Reform*. London: HMSO.

FURTHER READING FURTHER READING **FURTHER READING** FURTHER READING

Ann Hodgson and Ken Spours (2008) *Education and Training 14–19 Curriculum, Qualifications and Organisation*. Sage

This book focuses on the development of 14–19 education in this country and gives a clear history of developments throughout history.

Lumby, J and Foskett, N (2005) *14–19 Education.* London Sage.

Nicoll, K (2006) *Flexibility and Lifelong Learning.* Abingdon: Routledge.

Richard Pring et al (2009) *Education for All – The Future of Education and Training for 14–19 Year Olds*. Routledge

This book is good because it tries to consider what will happen in the future to 14–19 education and how things will change in reality.

Websites

See websites identified within the chapter.

8

Coming to the end of your assessed teaching

The objectives of this chapter

This chapter is designed to encourage you to develop your classroom teaching and to embrace the wider role of the lecturer in the PCET sector. The chapter considers how you can learn from your observations and feedback to ensure you are developing into an outstanding teacher and a reflective practitioner.

It addresses the following professional practice standards for QTLS:

AK 4.3 Ways to reflect, evaluate and use research to develop own practice, and to share good practice with others.

AK 7.3 Ways to implement improvements based on feedback received.

FK 2.1 Boundaries of own role in supporting students.

Introduction

> We are what we repeatedly do.
> Excellence then, is not an act, but a habit.
>
> Aristotle

As you are coming towards the end of your teacher training it is important to reflect on your learning so far, to consider the learning still to take place and to move towards a position of achievement and excellence in your practice.

Part of the process of undertaking this training is to demonstrate your own personal development over the course of the programme and to clearly track and evidence that progress. By completing your professional development files and reflective diary, you will have not only collected evidence of your achievements but reflected on them as well. The aim of this is to ensure you are fully aware of your own strengths and areas for improvement and are in a strong position when entering the job market.

Your ability to demonstrate your level of teaching skill, along with a detailed understanding of the wider role of the professional lecturer and an ability to be critically reflective, will ensure you are in the best position to gain employment in the PCET sector.

Tracking your achievements

Tracking your achievements is your own responsibility and includes the following.

- Tracking the achievement of your LLUK standards (see Appendix 3).
- Collecting evidence to demonstrate your achievement of the minimum core in literacy, numeracy and ICT.
- Completing your reflective diary.

- Collecting evidence to demonstrate your achievement of your individual development plan actions.
- Providing evidence of your relationship with your mentor.
- Providing evidence of your 150 hours of teaching, including lesson plans, resources, schemes of work as instructed by your place of study.
- Evidence of your eight observed sessions.
- Evidence of peer review and evidence of your having taken part in a range of teaching and explored the wider role of the lecturer.

One of the most essential things for you to do is to follow exactly the guidance given by your tutor and to start early.

A recent group of trainee teachers who were graduating were asked to produce their top ten hints for the new trainees. These were the following:

1. Keep on top of your personal development file.
2. Do a reflective entry in your diary every week.
3. Start reading as soon as possible.
4. Observe every lesson you can.
5. Try out activities seen in other people's classes.
6. Don't be afraid to ask for help from your mentor.
7. Plan your observations in good time.
8. Get up to date with technology.
9. Plan your workload and stick to your plan.
10. Get involved in your department and the wider role.

If you stick to these rules then you will be more likely to maximise your achievement and to get the most out of your course of study.

Learning from your observation

Here are some top tips to improve your teaching and learning.

- Be enthusiastic and make lessons interesting.
- Have activities that are suitable for all learners, whatever their age, ability and cultural background, and which are suitably demanding.
- Lead discussions to ensure that all learners have a chance to contribute and that they feel encouraged and valued.
- Give clear explanations, particularly of the links between theory and practice.
- Plan and prepare well so that you demonstrate accurate and up-to-date technical knowledge.
- Be sensitive to equal-opportunities issues.
- Make interesting use of ICT appropriate to the lesson.
- Make sure handouts are well produced and free from errors.
- Manage any change from individual to group work as smoothly as possible.
- Make sure you cover sufficient ground in the lesson and that learners achieve their objectives.
- Write clearly on whiteboards or overhead projectors.
- Use a range of methods to check that learning has taken place.

CASE STUDY

Teaching experience by Andrew – training to teach hospitality and catering

I am inspired by the journey that I have travelled as a student teacher. I reflect here for the last time on my Cert Ed course and I am amazed at how far I have come.

When I think back to my first observation, I think about how nervous I was and all the questions going through my mind. Will the students behave, be in on time, enjoy the session?

As I have developed as a reflective practitioner I have come to realise the students will only be as good as the person in front of them. If the resources are not up to scratch, or they do not allow for all the learners and correctly differentiate, then no amount of cajoling will keep them focused. Likewise, if the teaching environment is not suitable then the students will switch off.

My early observations were satisfactory. However, I have taken into account all of the areas identified by my observers and I have improved as a result of this. I have developed more resources that encourage students to be involved and designed activities that are appropriately challenging for all learners. I have learned to utilise self-directed learning and peer assessment and I have developed a wider understanding of questioning techniques.

My final observations were a lot better and I feel that all the hard work has resulted in tremendous developments in my practice.

One thing above all that has helped me is the great support I have had from my mentor, peers, tutors and colleagues. Without their support it would have been so different and I am truly grateful.

My favourite quote that I have found while completing this course sums up our role as lifelong learners and teachers.

> *Aim for success, not perfection. Never give up your right to be wrong, because then you will lose the ability to learn new things and move forward with your life.*
>
> Anonymous

REFLECTIVE TASK

1. Identify the ways in which you have improved since your first observation.
2. What else do you still need to work on?

The wider role – getting involved in your organisation

Identifying roles in the further education system

The learning and skills sector is diverse, and encompasses both teacher roles and teacher-related roles:

- *Full teacher roles:* LLUK research has identified a role which represents the full range of responsibilities performed by those who are expected to attain the status of Qualified Teacher, Learning and Skills

(QTLS). This role includes participation in activities such as pastoral support, assessment, internal verification, meetings and taking part in the quality-assurance systems of the organisation.

● *Teacher-related roles:* LLUK research has identified a role which contains limited teaching responsibilities. Examples of these include the role of professional assessor and a variety of other teacher-related roles, where elements of teaching are combined with elements of, for example, supporting other teachers and trainers. This can be through coaching, supporting learning, or management.

In order to gain QTLS you will need to take part in the full teacher role during your training. This means you will need to teach across a range of levels and groups as well as attend meetings, mark work, carry out support for learners and any other duties suggested by your mentor.

This may seem like a lot of extra work but it will hold you in good stead for interviews and for gaining employment within the sector. It is also important that you reflect on these wider duties in your journal and discuss them with your mentor.

One of the main things that new teachers say is that they find it hard to understand all the jargon and acronyms used in post-compulsory education and training (PCET). By immersing yourself in the department from the start, these will soon come to make sense to you and you will start to enjoy the experience.

Creating innovative resources and using new and emerging technology

As you develop as a teacher it is important that you investigate and develop your use of ICT and creative and innovative resources in your classroom. You will now be able to prepare and deliver basic teaching sessions and it is time to let your creativity loose in order to engage your learners and to unleash their learning potential.

There are many books available that give practical suggestions for activities (see further reading at the end of this chapter). Also you will find a vast number of websites that you can access to make resources and develop interactive activities.

The more variety you can use in the classroom, the more interested your students will be and the less likely you are to have any challenging behaviour.

Your ability to use ICT will depend on the facilities in your organisation, but it is important that you make maximum use of any technology that is available to you.

As in any area of activity, trying new things can go awry and it is important to keep a sense of humour about it and to have something available as a backup if all goes wrong on the day.

CASE STUDY

Preparing resources by Nicola – training to teach travel and tourism
This reflective account focuses on the range of resources and the innovative activities that I have developed during my teaching experience. The expanding choice of technology can be used by tutors to enhance and extend learning. It is important to relate to changes and advances that happen outside of the classroom and be adaptable and flexible in our delivery to reflect those changes.

> *Greater use of technology in education mirrors the greater use of technology in the home and the workplace.*
>
> (ILT and E-assessment, 2003, p116)

In light of these comments I have devised a research activity using ICT for my students. The benefits of using a variety of technological resources within the classroom are clear. It can enhance the interaction between the tutor and the students and provide a much wider variety of teaching and learning activities.

I have used technology to produce a number of creative resources including an interactive blockbuster quiz, quizzes, crosswords, word search, use of video and media clips, interactive drag-and-drop exercise and many others. The use of these resources has also removed some of the negative behaviour and has focused on developing more positive learning attributes among the students.

The use of creativity and ICT clearly links into my future development and will allow me to develop a more individualised approach to teaching and learning and to fully meet the needs of the many learners and learning styles I will come across.

PRACTICAL TASK PRACTICAL TASK PRACTICAL TASK PRACTICAL TASK PRACTICAL TASK

1. Do you use ICT in your sessions? Is there more you can do?
2. Use the internet to find and prepare an activity you have not used before.

CASE STUDY

Innovative teaching practice by Lorraine – training to teach psychology

It is generally noted that the use of innovative and creative resources within the classroom, particularly ICT, is an essential tool in creating a teaching environment that will impact on all learners (Neary, 2002, p28). Unfortunately I feel that the ICT and resources within the sixth form have been detrimental to the range of teaching methods that I have been able to employ within the classroom. Many of the classrooms within the sixth form are still lagging behind in the quality of innovative technologies that are employed within schools and other areas within the college.

During my first year of teaching I tried on a number of occasions to incorporate examples of ICT including YouTube and internet activities. Unfortunately on a few of these occasions the equipment/server failed to work and this left me very disappointed with the lesson and I was for some time reluctant to engage with this form of learning again.

However, during the second year of teaching, facilities within the college have improved and I have on a number of occasions used ICT to demonstrate theoretical concepts and experiments. I have used iPlayer to show new and up-to-date programmes that reinforce elements of the teaching matter. This was noted within my observation 7 whereupon the observer noted that the video clips *made interesting points that provoked a lot of discussion*.

Since attending a number of staff development days that emphasised the need for learner-led teaching, in which the teacher facilitated the activities rather than relying on more traditional didactic teaching methods, I have incorporated these methods on three separate occasions recently.

Students had to research how to demonstrate Piaget's theory of child development, design a poster and present their findings to their peers. The students were very competitive and really engaged with the activities, coming up with a number of innovative ideas that I had not envisaged. This creative method of teaching went so well that I have used this again on two separate occasions with different cohorts and different subject matter. This method of the learner-led teaching facilitated the ideals of an 'incorporative classroom', which encourages all learners *to act as a full participant in class activities and also feel themselves to be a valued member of the class* (Pollard, 2006, p132).

These activities also addressed the need for students to develop their presentation style. They were unaware that they would be required on that day to present and as such did not dwell too much on this; it also allowed them the opportunity to present with colleagues, which afforded them the confidence to initially present within a group.

As my current timetable incorporates a wide range of student cohorts ranging from GCSE to degree level I find it often difficult to judge if learners will be willing to engage with new and innovative teaching styles. As Rogers notes, *many student-learners will object to the teacher who abandons what they see as the traditional role of instructor and expert* (Rogers, 2007, p201) and this element of uncertainty for the engagement of the learners is what, in essence, makes teaching so exciting and challenging.

PRACTICAL TASK PRACTICAL TASK **PRACTICAL TASK** PRACTICAL TASK **PRACTICAL TASK**

1. Make time to go and observe other colleagues in your department – what can you learn from them?
2. Find out if there are any staff development sessions you can go on to develop your use of new and emerging technologies.

Ensuring an inclusive experience

Inclusion in further education (FE) is based on the concept of inclusive learning and not on the traditional discourse of inclusion/integration usually used in school education, which often involves notions of social acceptance and belonging.

Inclusive learning in FE was discussed by John Tomlinson in the Tomlinson Report 1996, a report published by the FEFC Learning Difficulties and Disability Committee. The concept is defined as follows:

> *Inclusive learning is a way of thinking about further education that uses a revitalised understanding of learning and the learner's requirements as its starting point. The aim is not for students simply to 'take part' in further education but to be actively included and fully engaged in their learning.*
>
> *By 'inclusive learning' therefore, we mean the greatest degree of match or fit between the individual learner's requirements and the provision that is made for them.*
>
> (FEFC, 1996, p32)

The report's proposals were aimed at improving FE's response to learners with disabilities or learning disabilities, and at matching provision to a wider range of individual learning needs.

It challenges the deficit model of the learner, and stresses the responsibility of the college or other educational institution to take into account the requirements of each individual.

'Inclusive learning' is a term designed to address the need to ensure that people can have access to further education and training, despite any learning or physical disability that they may have. The Tomlinson Report has been influential in promoting a learner-centred approach to further education and training which goes beyond the original remit of addressing the needs of people with learning difficulties and physical disabilities.

A key part of the report was that students with any learning difficulty or physical disability should not be seen as having problems, i.e. a deficit model, but to focus on what institutions could do to respond to their individual requirements. This approach should ensure that people are not labelled, and will be enabled to learn to the best of their abilities.

> *Put simply, we want to avoid a viewpoint which locates the difficulty of deficit with the student and focuses instead on the capacity of the educational institution to understand and respond to the individual learner's requirements and see people with disabilities and/or learning difficulties first and foremost as learners.*
>
> (FEFC, 1996, p2)

No longer would students be expected to adapt to the requirements of the currently constructed PCET institutions. PCET institutions would have to adapt to the needs of the learners coming through their doors. *Participation must be widened, not simply increased* (Kennedy,1997). This means that the curriculum offer is of paramount importance to encourage learners to participate.

> *It is arguably the curriculum which always stood – secure as a Berlin Wall – between mainstream and segregated special provision; it was the possibility of mediating that curriculum, and the means of its delivery, which enabled 'integrative' education; and it is still the curriculum on which the success of any truly inclusive initiative rests.*
>
> (Clough and Corbett, 2000, p21)

The terms 'widening participation', 'differentiation' and 'inclusive practice' are commonplace in the PCET sector. The PCET sector prides itself on its work in opening up opportunities for accessing education and training to a diverse population of learners. These concepts are defined as follows.

- 'Widening participation' is a process by which education and training providers take steps to recruit and then provide ongoing support to learners who due to their social, economic or ethnic backgrounds, are less likely to take part in education and training.
- 'Differentiation' is an approach to teaching and learning that both recognises the individuality of learners and also informs ways of planning for learning and teaching that take these individualities into consideration.
- 'Inclusive practice' is an approach to teaching and learning that endeavours to encourage the fullest participation of learners and that recognises and respects equality and diversity.

These three distinct concepts complement each other; it stands to reason that a widening participation approach will encourage an increasingly diverse learner population that will display a variety of different needs, and will therefore require an inclusive approach to planning for learning and teaching.

PCET institutions are vital in providing learners with the opportunities to participate on their own terms and to have their individual learning needs addressed. However, the quality of the experience that learners receive depends on the particular institution at which they study.

There is a massive variation in the opportunities offered and the extent to which individual institutions address the Tomlinson agenda. Some institutions reinforce the difference and provide negative experiences for learners whereas others enable learners to participate and to change their lives through quality education.

There are two approaches to coping with the inclusion agenda: either to try to help all learners to fit into the educational contexts they encounter or to try and adjust the educational environment to be more suitable for all the learners whose needs it is intended to address.

The second approach would be generally considered the most suitable. This would be all the more achievable by the industry continuing to think how best to design our learning environments to address the five factors that underpin successful learning.

In other words, inclusive teaching could be defined as doing everything we can to enhance the 'want' to learn and by adjusting the 'learning by doing' tasks and activities we use with learners, to allow all learners to have suitable opportunities to join in. We also need to maximise the 'feedback' that learners gain from us and each other and help all learners to 'make sense of' or 'digest' the information they encounter.

To achieve these aims we need to seek feedback from our learners about their experience of our teaching and their individual experience of learning in the context of their own particular needs. Learning is done by individuals; each learner learns in a particular way. Inclusive teaching is about helping all learners to optimise their own individual learning.

REFLECTIVE TASK

1. Identify the different groups of learners that you might encounter in your classroom. What internal and external factors might affect their learning?
2. What can you do to make them feel welcome in your classroom?

Example
You have just started teaching and been given your first tutor group. You have been given the following information about them.

They are studying for a level 1 introductory certificate in business. They will be taking basic skills in application of number, communications and IT and they are in class for four days a week – Friday being their day off.

- There are 16 in the class, 7 females, 9 males, 8 white, 6 Asian, 1 Angolan and 1 Chinese.
- The Angolan student is an asylum seeker who has been in the country for one year.
- One mature lady has two small children and is a single parent.

- One girl is in foster care and has no money.
- One boy has ADHD.
- One boy is hearing-impaired.
- Three of the students are Entry Level 2 in literacy.
- One girl was expelled from school for violent behaviour.

REFLECTIVE TASK

Consider what types of support would need to be in place to enable all of these students to achieve.

CASE STUDY

My own experience of teaching travel and tourism

There was nothing special about this travel and tourism tutor group, except for the students themselves. You could walk into any college anywhere and encounter a similar group.

I have chosen them from all the other groups I have taught because I liked them very much and grew to understand, with their help, that differentiation is not a concept to try to apply. It is a fact of life that we do anyway, completely instinctively in our everyday teaching.

There are 14 students in the group, one has Asperger's syndrome, one is partially sighted, two are mature students, one is Asian, two are dyslexic and one has been previously excluded from school for behavioural difficulties.

> *Differentiation is adopting strategies that ensure success in learning for all, by accommodating individual differences of any kind.*

> (Petty, 2004, p541)

Differentiation means recognising that each learner in the class differs in many ways. Once this has been recognised it is just a matter of planning each teaching and learning session, despite these differences, so that all of the learners learn and ultimately achieve their learning goals.

When you look at the individual profiles of the students in this class you begin to see and to understand the extent and complexity of each student's previous personal and educational experiences that have led to this point in their learning journey.

These students are studying for a BTEC National Certificate in Travel and Tourism (level 3) and are completing the second and final year. The course is assessed by coursework and is the equivalent to two A levels.

The teaching team are dedicated travel and tourism specialists with a wealth of industrial and teaching experience.

I taught this group for a year, Key Skills – Application of Number, and found that the results of diagnostic assessment meant I needed to deliver at level 1 and level 2 due to the ability level of the students.

I needed to use a range of teaching and learning strategies and to have activities available at the different levels. However, I was supported in my lessons by two learning support assistants, providing one-to-one support for individual learners.

It is impossible with a group like this not to adapt our teaching and learning style to compensate. The following are just a few examples.

Unless I was very clear and precise in my instructions then Garry would not be able to begin to work and would look bewildered and scared.

If I did not produce resources for the whole class in the font Arial 12 then Paul would not be able to see them and would be upset and feel as if he were being singled out.

If I used examples that were not culturally diverse and appropriate then Sima would feel isolated and excluded.

If I treated the class as children then Laura and Linda would feel excluded and disengage with the work.

If you teach maths as it is taught in schools then you lose the majority of the group who have had negative experiences. You need to teach application of number in a vocational context to re-engage those disenfranchised learners.

Once you have adapted your teaching style to suit the needs of the learners then it is easy to provide activities that differentiate between ability levels and allow students to learn at their own pace.

PRACTICAL TASK PRACTICAL TASK PRACTICAL TASK PRACTICAL TASK PRACTICAL TASK

1. Discuss this case study with your mentor – do you feel that this is a typical cohort?
2. Do you think having such a wide variety of students in one group works?

A SUMMARY OF **KEY POINTS**

In this chapter we have:

> **explored the full role of the lecturer in the PCET sector;**

> **discussed how you can improve your own practice based on your observed session and the feedback received;**

> **considered the issues involved in tracking your achievements;**

> **identified strategies that can be used to achieve your maximum potential.**

REFERENCES REFERENCES REFERENCES REFERENCES REFERENCES REFERENCES

Clough, P and Corbett, J (2000) *Theories of Inclusive Education: A Student's Guide.* London: Sage.

FEFC (1996) *Inclusive Learning: Report of the Learning Difficulties and/or Disabilities Committee.* London: HMSO.

Kennedy, H (1997) *Learning Works: Widening Participation in Further Education.* Coventry: FEFC.

Neary, M (2002) *Curriculum Studies in Post-compulsory and Adult Education.* Cheltenham: Nelson Thornes.

Petty, G (2004) *Teaching Today.* Cheltenham: Nelson Thornes.

Pollard, A (2006) *Reflective Teaching* (second edition). London: Continuum.

Rogers, A (2007) *Teaching Adults* (third edition). Maidenhead: Open University Press/McGraw-Hill.

FURTHER READING FURTHER READING FURTHER READING FURTHER READING

Andy Armitage et al (2007) *Teaching and Training in Post-compulsory Education*. Open University Press

> This book is good because it focuses on the full role of the lecturer and the industry in which they work. There are good examples and tasks for you to do to consolidate your learning.

Best, B and Thomas, W (2007) *The Creative Teaching and Learning Toolkit*. London: Continuum.

Eastwood, L et al (2009) *A Toolkit for Creative Teaching in Post-compulsory Education.* Maidenhead: Open University Press/McGraw-Hill.

Fisher, N (2007) *50 Templates for Improving Teaching and Learning.* Lewes: Connect Publications.

Ginnis, P (2002) *The Teachers Toolkit.* Carmarthen: Crown House.

Peter Scales (2008) *Teaching in the Lifelong Learning Sector*. Open University Press

> This book covers the full role of the lecturer in PCET and is a very useful basic textbook for trainee teachers. It is easy to read and full of useful tips.

Vickery, A and Spooner, M (2004) *We Can Work it Out*. Derby: Association of Teachers of Mathematics.

Websites

Brain boxx
> **www.brainboxx.co.uk**

Hot potatoes
> **www.hotpotato.com**

Puzzle maker
> **www.puzzlemaker.com**

9
Your triangulation meeting

The objectives of this chapter

This chapter looks at how you can prepare for the triangulation meeting(s) between yourself, the mentor and the observer from your teacher training provider. To do this it provides you with strategies on how to prepare yourself mentally, organise the appropriate paperwork and recognise what Ofsted grading criteria means to you in the context of your practice. To support this it details what you might be expected to contribute and what feedback you can expect. It will focus on examples of best practice and provide key tasks which offer you a framework for exploring the process and procedures at your organisation.

Throughout this chapter the word 'triangulation' will be used to describe the meeting between mentor, observer and trainee at specific crucial points of the programme. Other training providers will use different words to describe the same process.

It addresses the following professional practice standards for QTLS:

AK 4.2 The impact of own practice on individuals and their learning.

AK 4.3 Ways to reflect, evaluate and use research to develop own practice, and to share good practice with others.

AK 7.3 Ways to implement improvements based on feedback received.

BK 2.7 Ways in which mentoring and/or coaching can support the development of professional skills and knowledge.

BK 3.1 Effective and appropriate use of different forms of communication informed by relevant theories and principles.

CK 1.1 Own specialist area including current developments.

CK 1.2 Ways in which own specialism relates to the wider social, economic and environmental context.

DK 3.1 Ways to evaluate own role and performance in planning learning.

FK 4.2 Processes for liaison with colleagues and other professionals to provide effective guidance and support for learners.

Introduction

> *Education is the great engine of personal development. It is through education that the daughter of a peasant can become a doctor, that the son of a mineworker can become the head of the mine, that a child of a farm worker can become the president.*
>
> Nelson Mandela

A key feature of your professional practice module, and one that as a trainee teacher in the post-compulsory education training (PCET) sector you will identify as being of major importance in your professional development, is your assessment at the triangulation meetings.

The naming, timing and frequency of these meetings may vary according to the organisation in which you are placed or employed.

The parties involved in your interim and summative triangulation will usually include the people who have played a crucial role in observing and facilitating the development of your professional practice. The focus will be to discuss and agree your achievements, set targets for improvement and also identify your future continuous professional development (CPD) at the summative meeting.

Models of practice

Interim grading and triangulation

At the mid-point in your professional practice the supervising tutor and/or the mentor usually arrange an interim triangulation meeting, where a triangulation document will be completed. It may be you as the trainee who takes the lead and agrees a draft triangulation document with the mentor, before your supervising tutor's visit. The evidence will then be checked by the supervising tutor, who on talking to you will confirm (or amend) any judgements made. Outcomes from the interim meeting/grading will feed into a revised development plan.

Summative grading and triangulation

The summative triangulation takes place at the end of your placement. The decisions that are made are then recorded on a formal triangulation document.

The triangulation document may contain details of the subject and groups taught by you; it records achievements and targets against the LLUK standards; it also records an overall grade based upon the criteria specified in the document *Grading Initial Teacher Training 2008–2011*.

Remember

The triangulation meeting is very important because as well as recording your achievement against the professional practice standards for Qualified Teaching and Learning Status (QTLS), it summarises your strengths and areas for further professional development. This is often used as a basis for your personal tutor's/university's testimonial statement.

PRACTICAL TASK PRACTICAL TASK PRACTICAL TASK PRACTICAL TASK PRACTICAL TASK

Find out about the triangulation process that will affect you.

1. Who is involved in your triangulation?
2. Who sets up the date for the triangulation meeting?
3. Who completes the paperwork?

The Ofsted grading criteria and what they mean to you

The lesson observations that are carried out on you are conducted using the same common inspection framework criteria as Ofsted inspections and the same grading scheme.

PRACTICAL TASK PRACTICAL TASK PRACTICAL TASK PRACTICAL TASK PRACTICAL TASK

Read through Ofsted's grading recommendations.

These can be accessed at: **www.ofsted.gov.uk/Ofsted-home/Forms-and-guidance/Browse-all-by/Other/General/Grade-criteria-for-the-inspection-of-initial-teacher-education-2008-11**.

The grading scale identified in Chapter 2 may be applied to both your teaching observations and your summative triangulation grade.

PRACTICAL TASK PRACTICAL TASK PRACTICAL TASK PRACTICAL TASK PRACTICAL TASK

Prior to interim triangulation

1. Identify an area of your practice which you have worked to improve.

2. Now identify the areas of your practice you aim to improve in the next phase of your professional placement. Complete the action plan below.

Area for improvement	Action	People who can help	Target date

PRACTICAL TASK PRACTICAL TASK PRACTICAL TASK PRACTICAL TASK PRACTICAL TASK

Prior to summative triangulation

1. Identify how you have carried out the wider role in the Lifelong Learning Sector (LLS).

2. You may want to consider how as a teacher you have brought your own particular expertise to teaching and learning. How has this been utilised to contribute to:

   - developing opportunities for learner engagement outside the classroom. e.g. accompanying learners on trips to the cinema, theatre, museum, etc.?

   - working with other professionals, including those from multi-agency teams to ensure the needs of your learners are met, e.g. forming collaborations between careers advisors and your learners to facilitate the building of meaningful career pathways?

   - engaging with parents and carers to develop strategies to engage and motivate your learners to progress, e.g. partaking in parents' evenings for the 16–18 year old groups, which actively encourage their family to be involved in their child's progression routes?

CASE STUDY

A specialist in building and construction, Martin's experience

When I started my placement I was all set for going into the class and teaching. I did not really think about the wider role. My mind was full of how will I feel about standing up in front of a class? Will I freeze? What if I don't know the answers to the questions asked? However, the real challenges I faced were working effectively within a wider team of staff to make sure that the needs of my learners were met. For example, I taught a group of 15-year-olds who were on day release from school to study towards the new diploma in construction. In order to deliver a personalised approach I was encouraged by my mentor to have regular meetings with the link teacher from the school. Busy teaching all day in college, this sometimes meant having early morning or twilight meetings. I had to be flexible. The learners in question and their family members were also invited in order to have an input. Again flexibility was needed to ensure all could attend. At these meetings we would look at how the college and schools curriculum could link effectively to meet the diverse needs of the learner. It also gave the learner the opportunity to get involved and put their own goals and aspirations forward. This collaboration was not always straightforward because of the differing views about what should be taught. For example, I was keen for the vocational area to drive the lessons but the representative from school was keen to ensure literacy and numeracy were also taught. At times I was frustrated, I hadn't taught literacy and numeracy and could not see how they could be delivered effectively when I was teaching construction. It seemed it would have been so much easier to develop lessons without negotiation from the wider team. However, as soon I started to embed literacy and numeracy into my lessons it became so obvious how they can be linked to provide a more balanced approach to teaching and learning.

What's more, most of the learners from my group gained their vocational qualification and their level 1 in literacy and numeracy. This allowed them to progress onto the next level of the course and be a step closer to their goals of being qualified in a trade. Working in cross-collaboration partnership created an environment where important discussion about how to shape a fit for purpose curriculum could be created and helped me to develop my practice and way of thinking.

LLUK Professional Standards

The LLUK criteria will be used as a checklist to structure interim and summative assessment of your triangulation meetings and provide the basis for the overall grade. As such, an awareness of the standards is essential in identifying the areas you have excelled in, or need to address, in order to avoid failure and improve. Consideration of the standards will feed into your interim and summative review meetings with the supervising tutor.

PRACTICAL TASK PRACTICAL TASK PRACTICAL TASK PRACTICAL TASK PRACTICAL TASK

1. Interim – Look at the LLUK standards again and highlight any you have not addressed. From these choose three and consider how you aim to meet them effectively.
2. Summative – Now identify the strategies you have utilised in your pedagogy in order to meet six of the LLUK standards, e.g. using emerging technology, critical approaches to teaching and learning such as innovative curriculum design.

Remember

The standards are there as a guide; it is up to you to find exciting and meaningful ways to cover them. Be prepared to discuss the outcome of the above tasks at your triangulation meetings.

Preparing yourself mentally

Each of you will have different ways to prepare yourself mentally for the triangulation meetings. A good starting point is to consider your placement or place of employment and how it has shaped you as a professional. Partaking in a competency-driven teacher training framework and working within an often busy and demanding environment, will often include 'underground working' (see Gleeson, 2005), such as supporting learners' needs in unaccounted time slots like breaks and lunchtimes. This can often limit space for critical reflection and innovative practice. It can also lead to the temptation to adopt approaches which *reduce the role of teaching to that of a technical deliverer of pre-set pedagogies* (Brain et al, 2006). The teacher is viewed *as a machine* (Stronach et al, 2002), churning out prescriptive lessons rather than striving for new critical approaches which challenge you as a practitioner and your students. Crucially your autonomy and flexibility, both important in building and maintaining your professional integrity, can become compromised and eroded.

Therefore, early in your career it is worth developing strategies which enable you to find critical spaces to explore in meaningful ways both your professional identity and your practice.

If this is proving difficult, you may want to discuss your concerns with your mentor and tutor at your triangulation meetings. A step forward could be to build critical reflective tasks into the dialogue you have at your regular mentor meetings. At these meetings you may want to consider curriculum design and addressing the wider social and economic agenda of teaching and learning, rather than the narrow approach which assumes one size fits all.

> **CASE STUDY**
>
> **Ahmed, a specialist in engineering**
>
> Being a professional is about having the opportunity not only to share my subject specialism but also to utilise my skills in a wider way. This includes helping to break down the barriers to learning that students may face. To do this it was vital that I had the support of the mentor and the department to adapt the programme content and delivery to address the needs and motivations of my learners.
>
> To offer an example, initially a number of my learners, aged between 16 and 18 years, were convinced that they would never be able to pass the course. I wanted to raise their self-belief, confidence and aspirations. One action was building visits from former successful students and connections into the scheme of work. The former students were a real motivation while connections offered them insights into how to progress towards vocational routes of apprenticeships, jobs in the industry or to continue studying to a higher level.
>
> I also shared my own story. Having arrived at the very college where I now teach, without any qualifications, and worked my way up the exam system to achieve a degree, seemed to really inspire the learners. They told me that maybe it was possible that they could also go further than they had ever thought of before. To further raise

their aspirations I arranged for them to visit a local university. Here they watched a couple of sessions and spoke to the lecturers. When we returned to college we discussed the experience. This led to the entire group writing a five-year development plan. This they said was the first time they'd really reflected on their future; before it was more a case of see how it goes day to day. Over half the group plan to go to university, the others aim to complete apprenticeships. I got a great deal of satisfaction in helping the group to realise their potential. In order to do this it is vital that I have the space, support and strength to make teaching and learning meaningful to both myself and my learners. That is what being a professional is all about.

PRACTICAL TASK PRACTICAL TASK PRACTICAL TASK PRACTICAL TASK PRACTICAL TASK

1. How has the context of your professional placement shaped how you define yourself as a 'professional'?
2. Write a list of the strengths you have developed while on teaching practice.

You may have identified that you have:

- become more confident in your role;
- developed your use of questioning techniques;
- used more inclusive resources to motivate learners;
- used smarter targets when planning lessons;
- improved your timekeeping when delivering sessions;
- begun to embed functional skills successfully into your subject's specialist area;
- developed your voice projection so the clarity of your vocal delivery is clearer;
- used innovative pedagogical approaches;
- worked effectively in a multidisciplinary team;
- embedded ECM into the curriculum to meet individual learners' needs;
- become more critical in your reflections.

Part of being confident in the triangulation meetings is being equipped to answer any questions that might arise. To facilitate this it is a good idea to do the following.

- Make sure you are familiar with institutional policies and procedures, and find examples of where you have adhered to them.
- Ensure that you conform to appropriate LLUK professional standards.
- Find examples of critical engagement with your mentor. These may be recorded in your mentor log or your reflections.
- Find examples of where you have taken a full and active part in the wider aspects of a teacher's/ lecturer's role. This may include attending staff meetings, setting up pastoral activities such as lunchtime drama groups for the learners, developing and delivering curriculum packages across a range of learning needs.

Getting your paperwork together

Obviously, more will be expected of you as the programme progresses. This will be reflected in what you bring to the interim and summative triangulations.

REFLECTIVE TASK

1. What documents would you bring to the interim and summative triangulations?
2. How would they differ?

You may have considered the following:.

Interim	Summative
Initial Audit • This will identify the gaps in your knowledge and skills. Subsequently, an action plan will be compiled to address them within an appropriate timeframe.	**Initial Audit** • The gaps in your knowledge and skills should have been addressed at this stage. Evidence will need to be available that you have made progression.
Four teaching observation feedback forms (including two specialist).	Eight teaching observation feedback forms (including four specialist).
Personal development plan.	Updated personal development plan.
A reflective journal (on your learning and teaching) • Reflections in the journal may include: engagement with specialist mentor; integration of functional skills; subject specialist pedagogy; evidence of inclusivity, creativity, innovation and sustainability.	**An updated reflective journal demonstrating a deeper critical approach to practice** • Reflections in the journal may include the impact of engaging in the wider role of an LL tutor, e.g. widening the areas and levels you are teaching; more detailed specialised pedagogy, evidence of being able to work effectively on own initiative when delivering high quality lessons.
• The journal should refer to appropriate literature and be supported by evidence drawn from records of your specialist activity, e.g. lesson evaluations, lesson plans, records of specialist networking which may include your mentor.	• The journal should be more detailed and critical when referring to appropriate literature and be supported by evidence drawn from your specialist activity, e.g. lesson evaluations, lesson plans, and records of specialist networking and how you have engaged in the wider role of a tutor in the LLS.
Evidence that you are covering the minimum core which includes addressing your literacy, language, numeracy and ICT needs • E.g. if you arrived on the programme without a level 2 in literacy/numeracy, a target may be to achieve it. On achieving this you will need to include any certificate as supportive evidence.	**Evidence that you have completed the minimum core which includes addressing your literacy, language, numeracy and ICT needs** • This may be in the form of a booklet with each of the criteria signed off by your mentor/personal tutor. Again you will need evidence to accompany this which may include innovative resources you have developed which demonstrate your competence in ICT skills, etc.

LLUK Standards	LLUK Standards
• The LLUK criteria exist as a checklist which you would have covered in your teaching observations and practice. • It is expected that you will bring evidence of the LLUK standards you have met. You should have begun to track the LLUK standards you have covered.	• You should have completed all the LLUK standards. Your tutor and/or mentor may then sign them off to indicate that each one has been successfully achieved.
Draft interim triangulation document • You may have completed this with the mentor prior to the meeting.	**Draft summative triangulation document** • You may have completed this with the mentor prior to the meeting.
A log of your teaching or training hours • This will be approx. 75 hours at the midway stage.	**A log of your teaching or training hours** • This will be approx. 150 hours at the end of your placement.
Records of discussions with your mentor, including subject specialist issues. • This may include evidence of actions from the discussions.	**Completed records of discussions with your mentor, including subject specialist issues.** • This may include evidence that you have completed all the actions from the discussions, e.g. following accreditation guidelines, being actively involved in writing a new programme.
Assignment feedback • e.g. Preparing to Teach in the Lifelong Learning Sector (PTLLS).	**Assignment feedback** • e.g. Certificate to Teach in the Lifelong Learning Sector (CTLLS) and Diploma in Teaching in the Lifelong Learning Sector) (DTLLS).
Observations of experienced practitioners which include cross-context exchange opportunities. • Reflections on different approaches to teaching and learning.	**Observations of experienced practitioners which include cross-context exchange opportunities.** • Sharing of findings from critical reflection in community of practice.

What you might be expected to contribute

A key to recognising your development is to celebrate the distance you have travelled since commencing your teaching qualification. As part of your contribution you will be expected to discuss and show evidence of this development. It is worth being aware of your strengths and any areas of your practice you are seeking to develop and improve.

You might want to consider the following.

- How you have developed in your planning and preparation of your lessons.
- Show evidence that you have observed a wide variety of teaching in order to see how they manage different lessons in different curriculum areas.

- Demonstrate a clear understanding of how you have addressed and continued to review your targets for development over your professional teaching practice.
- Show how you have worked to develop an understanding of the needs of learners, including how you have provided learning experiences appropriate to diversity between individuals.
- Identify ways you have worked in a collaborative manner within the classroom and the wider college or training setting, utilising the skills of support staff and other members of the local and wider team.

At levels 6 and 7 you may consider the following.

- Highlighting how you are exploring critical pedagogical approaches. This may include addressing the politics embedded in your practices and recognising that pedagogy involves *a critical understanding of the social, policy and institutional context, as well as a critical approach to the content and process of the educational/training transaction* (Zukas and Malcolm, 2002, p215).

PRACTICAL TASK PRACTICAL TASK **PRACTICAL TASK** PRACTICAL TASK **PRACTICAL TASK**

1. Identify one area of your practice that has significantly developed.
2. Outline the key strategies you have put in place to develop it. Include reference to any support you have received from your mentor, personal tutor or wider team.

What feedback can you expect?

In both the interim and summative triangulations you can expect a rigorous assessment of your strengths and your areas for further development. This may include constructive criticism where clear and meaningful detailed targets are set for your development. The amount of targets set will vary, but it will be a number you can realistically achieve. An example of a summative feedback form is given in Appendix 5.

The feedback you receive may focus on the following.

- Achievements and targets detailed in your lesson feedback forms and your reflective portfolio.
- Knowledge and understanding of your subject area and pedagogical approaches.
- Concepts of educational psychology and how these are utilised in effective classroom delivery.
- Your understanding of the theoretical framework underpinning the learning process.
- Awareness and application of a range of models of curriculum analysis and development.
- Understanding of appropriate and meaningful methods of assessment and evaluation.
- Showing a deep awareness of a range of methods of educational enquiry in your teaching and training context.
- Your insight into equal opportunities and inclusivity in the LLS.
- How educational theory and practice apply to the context of your particular specialist teaching/training.
- Understanding of a range of contemporary developments and issues in post-compulsory education.
- The value of being a competent, reflective practitioner.
- The importance of communicating effectively with learners to facilitate learning.
- How you will take responsibility for your personal and professional learning and development.

The feedback you receive at your triangulations should be a dialogue, not a one-way statement, so ask questions as well as sharing your points with your mentor and tutor. They will identify how they have assessed you against the standards, particularly with regard to subject-specific teaching. This will culminate in the final assessment decision whereby a grading decision will be made.

If you are not making satisfactory progress and are deemed 'at risk', i.e. in danger of failing, different organisations will have their own procedure for dealing with this. You should familiarise yourself with the procedure so you are fully aware of all eventualities.

The crucial thing to bear in mind is that *Developing a professional approach goes beyond knowledge and skills to the core of personal growth and the ability to harness this growth into more effective action* (Beaty, quoted in Hall and Marsh, 2000, p17).

As such, in order to have progressed and achieved the LLUK standards you almost certainly will have built on your generic and subject-specialist practice. This may be significant in the development of more advanced strategies and methods for promoting learning which include a more detailed approach in specific specialist areas and their pedagogy. Underpinning this development will be your movement towards more critical reflections on teaching and learning, by recognising particular curriculum and professional challenges, and by developing informed responses to these concerns in critical, innovative, creative and meaningful ways.

A SUMMARY OF **KEY POINTS**

In this chapter we have:

> **discussed the Ofsted grading criteria and what they mean to you;**

> **explored how to prepare yourself mentally for the triangulation meetings;**

> **considered how to get your paperwork together effectively;**

> **examined what you might be expected to contribute;**

> **emphasised what feedback you can expect.**

REFERENCES REFERENCES REFERENCES REFERENCES REFERENCES

Beaty, L Becoming a Professional Teacher, in Hall, L and Marsh, K (2000) *Professionalism, Policies and Values*. London: Greenwich University Press.

Brain, K. Reid, I and Boyes, L (2006) Teachers as mediators between educational policy and practice. *Educational Studies*, 32(4): 411–23.

Brookfield, S (2006) *The Skillful Teacher: On Technique, Trust and Responsiveness in the Classroom* (second edition). San Francisco, CA: Jossey-Bass Wiley.

Gleeson, D (2005) Learning for a change in further education. *Journal of Vocational Education and Training*, 57 (2): 239–46.

Stronach, I, Corbin, B, McNamara, O, Stark, S and Warne, T (2002) Towards an Uncertain Politics of Professionalism: teacher and nurse identities in flux. *Journal of Educational Policy*, 17 (1): 109–38.

Zukas, M and Malcolm, J (2002) Pedagogies for Lifelong Learning: building bridges or building walls? in R Harrison, F Reeve, A Hanson and J Clarke (eds) *Supporting Lifelong Learning*. Vol. 1, *Perspectives on Learning*. Abingdon: Routledge.

FURTHER READING FURTHER READING FURTHER READING FURTHER READING

Clarke, A (2009) *The Minimum Core for Information and Communication Technology: Knowledge, Understanding and Personal Skills*. Exeter: Learning Matters.

Knud Illeris (ed.) (2009) *Contemporary theories of teaching and learning*. Routledge

This book has chapters by the key contemporary learning specialists of the day including Jack Mezirow and Howard Gardner. It is an excellent text that will encourage you to think beyond the traditional theories of teaching and enable you to develop your practice in the future.

Eric Sotto (2007) *When Teaching Becomes Learning*. Continuum

This book considers the power of learning in today's education system and encourages you to reflect on and reinterpret your own experiences.

Wallace, S (2007) *Teaching, Tutoring and Training in the Lifelong Learning Sector.* Exeter: Learning Matters.

Websites

Learning and Skills
   network www.lsnlearning.org.uk
Lifelong Learning UK
   www.lifelonglearninguk.org
NIACE
   www.niace.org.uk
Ofsted
   www.ofsted.gov.uk

10
Developing your career and applying for jobs

The objectives of this chapter

This final chapter focuses on your next steps in PCET. It provides you with approaches for your continuing professional development (CPD) while covering information on applying for jobs and preparing for that all-important interview. It also looks at moving on in PCET organisations and your career progression.

It addresses the following professional practice standards for QTLS:

BP 3.4 Evaluate and improve own communication skills to maximise effective communication and overcome identifiable barriers to communication.

CP 1.1 Ensure that knowledge of own specialist area is current and appropriate to the teaching context.

FP 3.1 Provide general and current information about potential education, training and/or career opportunities in relation to own specialist area.

Introduction

The wise teacher learns to work in effortless ways, doing things that come without stress.
They teach by doing what comes naturally.

Greta Nagal – *The Tao of Teaching*

CPD is important to anyone in a career that is always changing. Government agendas, practitioner research, and better understanding of the theories and practices of teaching will impact on how you meet the challenges that your role within the Lifelong Learning Sector (LLS) brings.

Engaging in meaningful CPD will facilitate your meeting these changes with integrity and confidence, while showing your ability and potential to future employers. This will empower you and open up opportunities for progression and career development.

This progression will be linked with critical reflection *to evaluate your experiences in order to facilitate your development as a teacher* (Gravells and Simpson, 2008, p98).

Within organisations there may be a dichotomy between what the college deems to be suitable CPD and what you feel would be beneficial for you. A college-driven approach can lead to a more remedial take on staff development where practitioners are viewed as the receivers of knowledge rather than the generators. To counter this I would recommend that you have a clear rationale to put forward when applying for courses or/and engagement in CPD.

Making a strong link to your practice is a good way to demonstrate the value of the CPD. You may be interested in practitioner research as a way to promote a deeper understanding and developing of your practice. Of course, what you choose will also depend on your aims and aspirations.

As teachers it is important to recognise that a number of professional standards, both statutory and advisory, apply to you at each point in your professional journey. Measuring yourself against these standards can help you benchmark your practice and, importantly, identify and address any learning and development needs. Effectively targeting, planning and managing your CPD can help you meet those needs, helping you to perform your role more effectively and providing you with the skills and knowledge you need to plug any gaps and to progress both personally and professionally.

Approaches to CPD

During your everyday practice you are probably carrying out more CPD than you imagined. This could be in the form of the books and/or professional journals you read to keep abreast of your subject-specialist knowledge, the reflections you make after your lessons and how these impact on future lessons, the meetings you attend, the conversations you have with colleagues regarding supporting learners, as well as training courses and network meetings you attend.

PRACTICAL TASK PRACTICAL TASK **PRACTICAL TASK** PRACTICAL TASK **PRACTICAL TASK**

Identify the activities you do that inform your practice.

Day	Activities
Monday	
Tuesday	
Wednesday	
Thursday	
Friday	
Weekend	

You may have considered:

- college appraisal meetings and how they feed into your development;
- cross-context observation of peers;
- attending staff meetings;
- being involved in a community of practice, e.g. Learning Skills and Research Network (LSRN);
- researching the new curriculum for your subject area;
- in-house training events;
- external training events.

The CPD activities are limitless and can be a mix of formal/accredited pathways. Importantly, the activities you choose should be relevant to you and your practice. You should critically reflect on what you have learned and show evidence of how this has impacted on you, your practice, your learners and the wider context in which you work, e.g. working within a multidisciplinary team.

Examples may stem from the exam results of your learners, their progression routes, their feedback, etc. An opportunity to discuss more formally your CPD and progress in your practice usually comes during your performance reviews. Even though the formality of these events can sometimes feel as though your professional development is being taken out of your control, it is important for you to maintain ownership.

As such you should equip yourselves with questions prior to going into the review and take notes of the outcome. This can promote dialogue which provides the basis for an empowering and enjoyable meeting rather than just being a case of you jumping through hoops to satisfy the powers that be.

REFLECTIVE TASK

As a practitioner in the LLS consider how you can update your teaching and learning methods and skills and your subject specific skills.

You may have considered:

- observing a peer;
- shadowing a work colleague;
- team teaching, e.g. workshops;
- joining a community of practitioners to share best practice;
- team self-assessment;
- subject learning coach training;
- peer coaching;
- updating knowledge through the internet/TV, e.g. Teachers TV, and reviewing these with a group of professional colleagues;
- partnership collaborations, e.g. schools, training providers, sixth forms, employers, etc.;
- e-learning activities;
- curriculum design, development, validation, implementation and review;
- reading about and engaging in practitioner research (see RaPAL and NRDC practitioner research for examples);
- partaking in accredited courses related to subject/vocational updating;
- membership of a specialised interest group;
- attending subject-specific conferences;
- subject learning coaching training;
- industrial updating through visits and placements;
- membership of professional bodies and societies in order to maintain or develop specialist vocational skills;
- reviewing books or articles;
- taking on examiner/verifier/assessor responsibilities;
- reading journal articles.

In order to keep yourself fully informed of the changes in the sector in which you work, it is essential that you are aware of the national policy initiatives and the wider context in which you are employed. These may include keeping updated on new policies/initiatives which relate to teaching such as the personalisation agenda, teaching for new curricula and qualifications such as 14–19 diplomas, equality and diversity training/updating and the impact on teaching, etc.

Recording your CPD

It is essential that you are rigorous in how you record your CPD. You will need to show evidence that you have critically reflected on what has been learnt, provide evidence on how the CPD has been applied to your practice, and how this has improved teaching and learning. Organisations will differ in the approach they advocate for collecting and recording evidence. Some provide annual portfolios so information such as attendance at training events, etc., can be collated. This file would then be taken to performance review meetings.

Throughout your teacher training programme you will have kept critical reflections. It is a good idea to continue doing this throughout your career. This is both good practice and will provide you with the opportunity to consider and explore how your knowledge and practice develop along your career trajectory.

The Institute for Learning (IfL) has developed Reflect (**http://reflect.ifl.ac.uk**), an online portal accessible via their website. Reflect provides a personalised learning space where you can reflect on your practice and record CPD. Enabling you to quickly and easily enter your CPD record, it can show and provide evidence that you have spent at least 30 hours each year (pro-rata if you are a part-time teacher/trainer with a minimum of 6 hours per year) on your CPD. For those of you newly qualified, recording your CPD allows you to complete the professional formation process and gain Qualified Teacher Learner and Skills (QTLS) or Associate Teacher Learning Skills (ATLS) status.

This formal recognition of your full professional status, issued by IfL, positions you on a par with other professionals. This a stride forward in achieving equality of esteem and mutual recognition of status between school teachers and those working in the Lifelong Learning Sector. Thereby, teaching in the LLS is viewed as a career of choice, considerable value and worth, rather than being seen as what historically has been the Cinderella of the education sector.

PRACTICAL TASK PRACTICAL TASK PRACTICAL TASK PRACTICAL TASK PRACTICAL TASK

Using 'Reflect', select the most effective way for you of recording your CPD. For support in the process you may want to go to:

http://www.pebblelearning.co.uk/reflect/Connections/Tipsheets/Creating%20a%20CPD%20 record.pdf

Now start/complete your IfL CPD record.

Academic pathway

On your successful completion of the teaching qualification, dependent upon your academic profile you may want to progress onto the following pathway:

Cert in Higher Education in PCET (level 5)

⇩

Foundation Degree In Teaching in the Lifelong Learning sector

⇩

BA (Hons) in Education and Training

⇩

MA in Education/PCET PGCE students (level 6/7) start here

⇩

(EdD)/PhD Doctor of Education

Figure 10.1 Academic pathway in teaching

Joining a group of like-minded practitioners

In a busy department where you are heavily timetabled, it can sometimes become isolating. Joining a community of practice is an excellent way to meet other practitioners and share best practice. Communities are usually groups of people who share a commitment and passion about a topic and who strengthen their knowledge and expertise by engaging on an ongoing basis (Wenger et al, 2002). The groups do not have to be work colleagues. The social practice of learning is celebrated in the group.

An example is Dialogue North West: **www.lancs.ac.uk/dialogue_nw/contacts.htm**

> *The aim of Dialogue North West is to create a forum where individuals and organisations in the North West can share and develop research and practice in adult literacy, numeracy and ESOL. In doing this, it encourages the development of research by establishing networks and circulating information. The research forum welcomes practitioners, providers, policy makers and researchers to take part in discussion, seminars, professional development opportunities and training events. The Dialogue North West steering group is made up of a diverse range of individuals and organisations involved in the learning and skills sector, and the group is co-ordinated by the Lancaster Literacy Research Centre.*
> Accessed from: **www.lancs.ac.uk/dialogue_nw/index.htm**

Applying for jobs

For most pre-service trainees, in addition to the final objective of achieving the award of QTLS the ultimate goal at the end of the programme is to secure a teaching post. For in-service trainees succeeding in the course means they are open to other opportunities which include career progression.

Applying for jobs can be an anxious time and one where commitment to succeeding is vital. I have seen trainees apply for a number of jobs before being accepted, but it is this determination that has landed them employment. The key is do your research and not give up.

REFLECTIVE TASK

Consider what research you could be conducting for jobs in your specialist area.

Jacqui Howe is Head of Careers at Edge Hill University and works closely with tutors in the Faculty of Education to help trainees obtain their first teaching post. The Careers Centre each year organises a Teaching Fair – nationally regarded by many as the best in the country – and Jacqui has a wealth of experience of recruiting and interviewing for teaching posts. Below she outlines some tips.

Tips for obtaining your teaching/lecturing post or how to get that job.

1. Find out what support your university careers service can give you and use them. Do they organise a teachers' fair for you? Is there information on their website or do they operate a teaching vacancy service? Can they give you individual help with teaching applications or offer workshops? Ask the questions and use the support.
2. What specific help with job applications can the tutors on your course give you? Find out what support there will be and make sure that you do not miss out on it.
3. Decide geographically where you want to work and start looking out for vacancies on general websites such as **www.fejobs.com** or on individual college/other organisations' websites. It is never too early to start looking. If you are on a one-year full-time programme which started in September, you should be looking from December onwards. It may sound early but some lecturing posts will be advertised early and there is less competition the earlier you apply.
4. Put together a two-page teaching CV which gives your contact details, teaching and degree/professional qualifications and your teaching experience first – starting with your most recent qualifications and experience.
5. Do your research on the organisation you are applying to – look for something that you can put in your opening paragraph to show how much you want to work for – or would fit into – the organisation you are applying to.
6. Your letter of application – always think about what you are compiling from the employer's point of view and what they want to know. Most organisations use person specifications and you need to use this as the framework for your application. If possible, address the criteria in the order they were given to you – make it easy for the recruitment panel to find their criteria and your evidence of how you match these criteria.

PRACTICAL TASK PRACTICAL TASK PRACTICAL TASK PRACTICAL TASK PRACTICAL TASK

1. Find a job vacancy and send for the application form.
   You might want to visit the following websites: **www. fejobs.com**, **www.tes.co.uk/**
2. Complete the application form and covering letter.

You should consider:

- Correct grammar and punctuation.
- Selling yourself. This includes using strong adjectives to describe your skills.
- Ensuring your skills match the person specification.

- Complete in draft. Ask someone to check it before you send it off. A second pair of eyes can often spot easy-to-miss mistakes.

You may also emphasise more general transferable skills such as:

- time management;
- organising your work;
- meeting deadlines;
- working as part of a team.

CASE STUDY

Applying for jobs – Kevin teaching law

For me the quest for employment started around mid-February when advertisements for posts commencing in September started to appear. Along with most of my colleagues I started to look (usually each Friday) at the TES website and other websites such as **www. fejobs.com**.

Having identified a potential post I then started a process of research. It would be good to say that the purpose of this research was to form an opinion which would guide a decision as to whether I would like to work for the organisation advertising the post and whether the remit of the post advertised was something which attracted me. However, like most students, I suspect, I would have to say that, in the present economic climate, I was prepared to apply for any post (within reason). The objective of initial research was therefore to gain knowledge about the post and the employing organisation which would help me with the application process. For example, I wanted to know about the ethos of the college. Were there any features of my prior work and life experiences and qualifications which, if emphasised on the application form, would make me more attractive to the college? Were there any features of the curriculum offered by the college in my subject which could be matched to particular aspects of my experience and which could be exploited by me in the application process? I thought that time spent on this research would be time well spent in improving my attractiveness and potential utility to employers. Of course, I could have jumped straight into completing the application process, but unless you know what sort of teacher an employer is looking for, how can you try to prove that you are that teacher?

Before I was successful in securing a post, I applied for five positions and was shortlisted and interviewed for four of them. The application process in all of these cases was the same. A copy of your CV is never required. Instead, you are required to complete the college's standard application form, supplying the standard biographical details, a list of your qualifications and the dates obtained and details of your previous employment experience with employers' names, posts held and responsibilities.

In addition, the applications all required submission of a personal statement, or similarly named section of the application form, in which you were asked to show how you met the requirements of the person specification for the post. In my experience, the person specification and the personal statement are the key documents in any application process. The person specification tells the applicant exactly what the employer is looking for. In most cases the specification is set out in terms of 'essential criteria' and 'desirable criteria'. The essential criteria are those qualifications, features of experience, or abilities which are essential to the post. So if you haven't got them, or, more importantly, can't show that you have them, you will not even be considered for an interview. One of the management team at my placement college told me that they use the essential criteria on the person specification as a set of 'tick boxes'. Very often this is done by a person in the HR Department who reads through the personal statement to see if they can tick all the boxes. If they cannot, then the candidate is not shortlisted. If they can tick all the boxes then they are supposed to offer you an interview.

With this in mind, before I started completing a personal statement, I sat down and looked in detail at the person specification for the post. Firstly, how could I show that I met the essential criteria? Could I tick all the boxes? Some boxes can be ticked without much thought. If one of the essential criteria is 'at least a level 4 qualification in XYZ' then you have either got this or you haven't.

Other essential criteria take a lot more thought. 'Ability to work as an effective member of a team', for example, requires not just thinking about whether you can work as an effective member of a team, and stating that, but requires you to think about how you can prove that you can work as an effective member of a team. Therefore, 'I am able to work and committed to working as an effective member of a team' is no good and I knew that I needed to think of specific examples of times when I had worked effectively in a team or aspects of previous employment in which effective team working was essential. So, for example, I may have written, 'Working as a nurse on a busy hospital ward demands the ability to work as an effective member of a team which consists of doctors, nurses, physiotherapists, pharmacists, all working together to ensure the best standard of treatment and care for patients. In this role I was responsible for ensuring that records were kept and details about responses to treatment were communicated to other colleagues within the team. Without my contribution the team would not have functioned successfully.'

In my personal statements, when thinking about examples, I included not only examples taken from previous employment, but also examples from other life experiences. I think that the rule is that any experience, as long as it is relevant to the essential criterion under consideration, is valuable and can be cited in one's personal statement.

I found that, as many person specifications tend to require the same essential criteria, once you have come up with a personal statement which adequately addresses those criteria it may just be a matter of juggling around your examples of how you meet the criteria. Of course, in drafting a personal statement, one could end up including too much information. In the applications which I submitted, I made sure that my personal statement was no more than two sides of A4.

For a number of trainees the opportunity to secure employment sometimes arises from their teaching practice placement. As such it is worth showing the team how committed you are. Get involved in all aspects of the programme, including attending meetings and pastoral activities such as trips to the theatre with groups of learners. This not only gives you the opportunity to be involved in the wider role, it also offers you the chance to get noticed as someone who is willing to go that extra distance. Never underestimate the importance in letting the organisation know you are enthusiastic and committed – both are assets that will be sure to impress.

Going for the interview

So you're over the first hurdle. Shortlisted for the job, now it's time to prepare for the interview. The end result is the job you want. The better you prepare, the more chance you have of impressing the interview panel. Your objective is to succeed. How are you going to do this? You need to know what might come your way. You need to demonstrate that you know about the organisation you are applying to, know about the position, know how to do the job and let the interviewers know you would be the best person for the job.

Therefore, the key is to be prepared for the interview and all it brings. There are a number of factors you must take into account, the first being that you are not late for the interview. If you are applying for a job at a PCET provider some distance away, plan your route, doing a practice to get the timings right if necessary.

For those of you who are in-service you may be applying for an internal job. It is essential that you also make sure that you prepare well. Yes, you may know the organisation well but there will be others who apply and these could be external and also bringing many skills.

The interview is the most important part of the job-seeking process. Here your preparation will pay dividends. Surrounded by strangers who are putting questions to you, the interview can be the most stressful time. You need to keep your focus.

REFLECTIVE TASK

Consider some of the questions you may be asked at the interview.

In terms of questions asked at interview, trainees' feedback often indicates that they fall into two broad categories: questions about teaching and learning, and questions about their abilities to contribute to the life of the organisation. The following themes appeared to be favourites on the teacher's role within the life of the college.

- Why have you applied for this job?
- How could you support/contribute to the mission/ethos of the college?
- What qualities/attributes/skills would you be able to offer the college and your learners?
- What qualities/attributes/skills does/should a good teacher have?
- Questions about your relationship as a teacher with your line manager or team leader.
- How would you promote the image/reputation of the college or 'sell' the college to prospective students?
- Why do you want to be a teacher (in general), and here at this college (in particular)?

In terms of questions about teaching and learning, common questions involved these themes.

- Tell us about the knowledge and skills you are bringing to the role.
- How do you deliver personalised approaches to teaching learners?
- Strategies to motivate learners.
- Strategies for differentiation (not only to accommodate more able and less able learners, but also to accommodate learners of *average* ability).
- Strategies for managing behaviour.

- What do equality, diversity and inclusion mean to you and what strategies would you adopt to promote them?
- Strategies for embedding functional skills.
- Strategies for promoting Every Child Matters.

You may be given scenarios where you need to identify what you would do. An example is:

> You have a group of 16-year-olds who are studying health and social care. Two members of the group start arguing with each other and disrupting the rest of the group. What strategies do you use to deal with the situation?

Reading the list, trainees often have the feeling that it should be easy for anyone following a PGCE/CertEd programme to discuss those themes in detail. However, what many interviewers are looking for are specific examples of how you have had to manage behaviour or how you have differentiated or embedded functional skills. *Think of a lesson which you have delivered which went particularly well. Why did it go well?* Sit down and look at the lessons which you have delivered during your placement to identify those specific examples which the interviewers seemed to want. This will help you feel much more confident about answering these sorts of questions.

You may also be asked to prepare a mini lesson for the interview. This is your opportunity to shine. If it's for 20 minutes you don't do a one-hour plan. Have clear aims and objectives. If possible, relate your lesson to best practice such as embedding Every Child Matters and embedding functional skills. Make it interesting; don't just read from a PowerPoint presentation. Practice beforehand so you get the timing right and you know the content fully. If needs be, ask a colleague to check over your paperwork and listen to you. You could also ask your mentor for their input.

CASE STUDY
Kevin shares his interview preparation

I received four invitations to go for interview and in each case the format for this part of the selection procedure was fairly similar. I was asked to attend for 0830 or 0900 on the appointed day. During the day, I would be required to deliver a microteaching session of 20 minutes duration, on a topic selected by the college, to a group of students who were currently enrolled at the college. In addition, the day would feature at least one interview. In some cases the microteaching brief required me to produce and submit a lesson plan. In other cases it did not mention a lesson plan. However, I always prepared and submitted a lesson plan for the observers of the lesson.

Preparation for the interview day was therefore time-consuming and in each case took me at least a whole working day. Preparation for a microteaching session is perhaps more difficult than for a full one-hour lesson. In some cases I was asked to prepare the full one-hour or two-hour lesson but to deliver just the first 20 minutes. In other cases I was asked to prepare a lesson lasting just 20 minutes. Your approach has to be dictated by the brief given, but I felt it necessary to show what I could do in terms of good practice in teaching and learning and therefore I wanted to present a lesson which would engage and motivate learners, which would differentiate between more able and less able learners, which would be inclusive of differing learning styles and learning needs and, of course, which would cover everything which the brief demanded.

I used the lesson-plan template which I used for my teaching and learning observations on placement. This helped me ensure that I had included all the appropriate items in my 'teacher's toolkit'. I knew I had to include an activity to engage learners, and other teaching and learning strategies which would accommodate the other things which I wanted to achieve in the lesson – all in 20 minutes.

The phrase 'death by PowerPoint' will be familiar to many students. However, I used PowerPoint in all my microteaching sessions and I think that the important thing about PowerPoint is to make it work for you, as an adjunct to teaching and learning, rather than to allow it to dominate your lesson and therefore create constraints to what you want to do. In case the ICT facilities were conspiring against me on the day, I always had a 'plan B'. In addition, I felt that it looked good if I could turn up not only with impressive resources (with two or three packs, including the lesson plan and resources, for the observers) which enhanced teaching and learning, but also with incidental things such as pens and paper for learners who may not have brought them to the microteaching session, adhesive labels or tent cards on which learners could write their names and marker pens for the same purpose and for writing on the whiteboard if needed.

So, preparing my lesson took up a fair amount of time. The rest of preparation time for an interview was taken up with researching the organisation and trying to anticipate questions which would be asked. Researching the organisation is obviously important. At every interview I was asked how I felt I could contribute to the mission or the ethos of the college – obviously difficult to answer if you don't know what the mission or the ethos of the college is. Interviewers also seemed to be impressed when I was able to discuss a few points made by the most recent Ofsted report on the college or quote the college's examination result record.

In at least one interview I was asked about the features of the examination board specification for law which was taught at the college. I was therefore pleased that I had looked in some detail at that particular board's specification. Another source of questions was my potential contribution to the college's enrichment activities and it was therefore good to know what activities the college already pursued. Most of this information was to be found on the various colleges' websites.

It can be very disappointing if you are given the news you have been unsuccessful in securing the position. However, it is in your own interest to receive feedback on your interview performance. Most feedbacks are given over the phone and it is worth taking notes which you can refer to. Any areas for development can then be followed for the next interview. The key is not to give up.

Moving on in PCET

There are lots of opportunities for progression in PCET. An awareness of the avenues you can travel can help you plan your career journey. Of course the paths you take may follow different routes than anticipated. What's certain is that the skill, knowledge and experience you gain will equip you to travel along different routes with confidence and professionalism. Your journey may lead to your taking on the role of sharing best practice and disseminating your knowledge and skills to colleagues in roles which include:

- professional mentor;
- advanced practitioner;
- specialist teaching and learning coach;
- curriculum leader;
- internal verifier.

Your journey's cycle

The LLUK (2006, p4) recommends that programmes of CPD activities should be planned on the basis of 3/5-year cycles with an annual programme of activity. This model allows you to plan for your future development.

It is worth talking this through at your performance review as this will offer you the opportunity to ascertain whether funding is available to pay for external courses/training. However, planning in a linear way may mean there are potential restrictions related to professional learning. Important knowledge related to professional practice can often be emergent and so is difficult to predict. This unpredictability should be built into your planning, offering you the space to explore your needs rather than limit the possibilities. It is these possibilities that lie ahead and by embracing them you can move forward both personally and professionally.

A SUMMARY OF **KEY POINTS**

In this chapter we have:

> **explored what happens when you gain your teaching qualification;**

> **considered your future CPD;**

> **discussed applying for jobs in the LLS;**

> **addressed preparing for your interview;**

> **considered moving on in PCET.**

REFERENCES REFERENCES REFERENCES **REFERENCES** REFERENCES REFERENCES

Gravells, A and Simpson, S (2008) *Planning and Enabling Learning in the Lifelong Learning Sector*. Exeter: Learning Matters.

LLUK (2006) *Sharing of Good Practice in Professional Development among Staff in Further Education and Work-based Learning*. London: LLUK.

Wenger, E, McDermott, R and Snyder, WM (2002) *Cultivating Communities of Practice*. Boston, MA: Harvard Business School Press.

FURTHER READING FURTHER READING **FURTHER READING** FURTHER READING

Cross, S (2009) *Adult Teaching and Learning: Developing your Practice*. Open University
    This is a good book to have at hand. It explores the role of the teacher and how to shape the lesson. It offers meaningful approaches which help you to reflect and build on your own practice.

Hitching, J (2008) *Maintaining Your Licence to Practise*. Learning Matters.
    Meaningful and relevant activities for practitioners across the sector.
    This provides some very good activities for prompting meaningful CPD which links clearly to reflection. It provides a clear picture of meeting the requirements of fulfilling your licence to

practise. A good one to dip into on your break times at work.

Lea, J et al (2007) *Working in Post-compulsory Education*. Maidenhead: Open University Press/ McGraw-Hill.

Lumby, J (2001) *Managing in Further Education*. London: Sage.

Websites

Education jobs
   www.educationjobs.com
FE Jobs
   www.fejobs.com
Institute for Learning
   www.ifl.ac.uk
Learning and Skills Research Network
   www.lsrn.org.uk/allcontacts
NRDC
   www.nrdc.org.uk
North West Dialogue
   www.lancs.ac.uk/dialogue_nw/about.htm
Reflect
   www.reflect.ifl.ac.uk
TES
   www.tes.co.uk/jobs
The Excellence Gateway
   www.excellencegateway.org.uk

Appendix 1

Scheme of work

Organisation:

Course:

Section/Department:

Unit/Module:

Year:

Awarding body	Course code/identifier
Level of course entry requirements	External assessment requirements and dates (e.g. exams, coursework)
Duration and end date of course Duration and end date of unit/module	External verifier or coursework moderator Name and contact details (as applicable)

	Mode of attendance	FT/PT
Overview of learner cohort: number, gender, age, ethnicity		
Specific learning support needed	Support provided through… Support staff names and contact details	
Preferred learning styles identified	Strategies to incorporate PLS into delivery	
Additional information about course of learners		

(Continued)

Appendix 1 *(Continued)*

Week/date	Topic and learning objectives (students will be able to …)	Teaching and learning strategies	Resources	Assessment

Appendix 2

Session Plan

Course	
Session title	
Week no/date	
Time	
Duration	
Location	
Tutor/s	
Aims	
Objectives	
Differentiated learning	

(Continued)

123

Appendix 2 *(Continued)*

Notes						
Resources to be booked						
Information for learners						
Learner needs						
Learning support						
Assessment updates – hand in/returns						

Functional skills (key skills)			
English (communication)	Maths (application of number)	IT	Every Learner Matters (ECM)
			Wider key skills

Appendix 2 *(Continued)*

Approximate timings	Learning objectives	Learner activity	Teacher activity	Resources	Assessing learning

(Continued)

Appendix 2 *(Continued)*

Evaluation	
Individual targets for improvement	1. 2. 3. 4. 5.

Appendix 3

LLUK Professional Practice Standards Tracking Sheet

Professional values and practice	Learning and teaching	Specialist learning and teaching	Planning for learning	Assessment for learning	Access and progression
AP 1.1	BP 1.1	CP 1.1	DP 1.1	EP 1.1	FP 1.1
AP 2.1	BP 1.2	CP 1.2	DP 1.2	EP 1.2	FP 1.2
AP 2.2	BP 1.3	CP 2.1	DP 1.3	EP 1.3	FP 2.1
AP 3.1	BP 2.1	CP 3.1	DP 2.1	EP 2.1	FP 3.1
AP 4.1	BP 2.2	CP 3.2	DP 2.2	EP 2.2	FP 4.1
AP 4.2	BP 2.3	CP 3.3	DP 3.1	EP 2.3	FP 4.2
AP 4.3	BP 2.4	CP 3.4	DP 3.2	EP 2.4	
AP 5.1	BP 2.5	CP 3.5		EP 3.1	
AP 5.2	BP 2.6	CP 4.1		EP 3.2	
AP 6.1	BP 2.7	CP 4.2		EP 4.1	
AP 6.2	BP 3.1			EP 4.2	
AP 7.1	BP 3.2			EP 5.1	
AP 7.2	BP 3.3			EP 5.2	
AP 7.3	BP 3.4			EP 5.5	
	BP 3.5				
	BP 4.1				
	BP 5.1				
	BP 5.2				

KEY

01	Tutor observation 1
02	Tutor observation 2
03	Tutor observation 3
04	Tutor observation 4
S1	Subject mentor observation 1
S2	Subject mentor observation 2
S3	Subject mentor observation 3
S4	Subject mentor observation 4

Appendix 4 Example observation feedback

Feedback comments should identify and consider the following points as appropriate:

Effectiveness of teaching, training and learning: planning (including differentiation), knowledge of learners; addressing the full range of learners' needs including challenge; meeting course requirements; use of resources, use of e-learning, quality of communication; subject-specific expertise – knowledge, enthusiasm, linking theory/practice; teaching of key skills; evidence of teacher's personal skills in the minimum core.

Achievement of learners: suitability and use of assessment; standard of learners' work; evidence of progress relative to prior attainment, initial assessment and potential (value added and distance travelled); learners' attendance, engagement, enjoyment; acquisition of workplace skills.

Meeting needs and interests of learners: learners are on an appropriate programme; teacher is aware of learner expectations; programme and teaching show an awareness of issues to be addressed under Every Child Matters.

Guidance and support: There is evidence of care, guidance and support to safeguard welfare and promote personal development.

The lesson was very well planned with a detailed scheme of work that clearly identified assessment opportunities and linked to the AAT devolved assessments. The lesson plan was detailed and linked in Every Child Matters themes, and opportunities to assess key skills were identified.

Aims and objectives were differentiated and shared with learners at the start and end of the session. Evidence in student work files shows they are developing the necessary accounting skills, and that underpinning knowledge is being delivered and assessed.

The recap activity at the start tested students' understanding of capital and revenue expenditure, with students having to hold up a laminated card to identify if the example given was a capital or revenue expense, and either a debit or credit entry. However, the adult students did not seem to enjoy this activity and it was cut short.

Lesson materials were produced to a high quality and an excellent PowerPoint presentation with video clips explained the concept of social accounting. An innovative use of scenarios was used to test students' understanding of the financial and social costs, and benefits of companies' decisions. The scenarios were challenging and provoked discussion and debate within the groups. Be careful to ensure scenarios provide an equal opportunity for all students to join in. Some students were not always clear about the distinction between social and environmental issues.

Directed questioning was used to check understanding and mini whiteboards were used to provide variety and to test the understanding of all students.

Students demonstrated good understanding of the principles of social accounting and how it links to double-entry bookkeeping.

The summary at the end was clear and gave students the chance to identify areas they were not sure about by using sticky notes. Homework was set and a brief introduction to next week's session was given. The objectives were revisited and checked off.

Record of LLUK Professional Practice Standards evidenced

Professional values and practice		Learning and teaching		Specialist learning and teaching		Planning for learning		Assessment for learning		Access and progression	
AP 1.1		BP 1.1	Y	CP 1.1		DP 1.1	Y	EP 1.1		FP 1.1	
AP 2.1		BP 1.2		CP 1.2	Y	DP 1.2	Y	EP 1.2		FP 1.2	
AP 2.2		BP 1.3		CP 2.1	Y	DP 1.3		EP 1.3		FP 2.1	
AP 3.1		BP 2.1	Y	CP 3.1	Y	DP 2.1		EP 2.1		FP 3.1	
AP 4.1		BP 2.2	Y	CP 3.2		DP 2.2		EP 2.2		FP 4.1	
AP 4.2		BP 2.3		CP 3.3		DP 3.1		EP 2.3		FP 4.2	
AP 4.3		BP 2.4		CP 3.4		DP 3.2		EP 2.4			
AP 5.1		BP 2.5		CP 3.5				EP 3.1			
AP 5.2		BP 2.6		CP 4.1				EP 3.2			
AP 6.1		BP 2.7		CP 4.2				EP 4.1			
AP 6.2		BP 3.1						EP 4.2			
AP 7.1		BP 3.2						EP 5.1			
AP 7.2		BP 3.3						EP 5.2			
AP 7.3		BP 3.4						EP 5.5			
		BP 3.5									
		BP 4.1									
		BP 5.1									
		BP 5.2									

Comments on specific standards as evidenced

Your knowledge of accounting is current and appropriate to the teaching context. You used appropriate and innovative ways to enthuse and motivate learners about accounting and applied appropriate strategies and theories of teaching and learning.

Current strengths

- A well-planned and resourced session that clearly encouraged students to learn and enjoy the subject.
- Innovative activities were used effectively to ensure all students contributed and were able to illustrate and compare social accounting and financial accounting.
- Challenging scenarios were used for the group task to stimulate discussion.
- Some good evidence of attainment – students demonstrated good understanding of the principles of social accounting.

Targets for development

- Consider the appropriateness of the card activity for your group of adult students.
- Ensure equal opportunities are considered when designing scenarios.
- Clarify the distinction between social costs and environmental costs to ensure students have a clear understanding of the difference.

Appendix 5 An example of a completed summative feedback document

LLUK Professional Standards

Domain A Professional values and practice	Achievements Excellent relationship with all the team. Very responsive to suggestions and recommendations. Strong link between theory and practice, demonstrated clearly in outstanding lessons and innovative practice. Targets/Action To continue to reflect and develop practice.
Domain B Learning and teaching	Achievements A highly effective communicator who has consistently delivered differentiated lessons to promote an inclusive approach. This has motivated the learners and can be clearly demonstrated in the high retention and achievement. Confident use of a wide range of high standard materials and resources. Targets/Action To continue to develop effective strategies for teaching and learning.
Domain C Specialist learning and teaching	Achievements Wide and detailed command of specialisms within law. Complex principles delivered in a manner which links your work practice to the issues, rather than presenting decontextualised theory. Targets/Action Attendance at/inclusion in appropriate updates.
Domain D Planning for learning	Achievements A very good differentiated delivery determined by the ability and culture of a diverse cohort of learners. Targets/Action
Domain E Assessment for learning	Achievements Most responsive to suggested targets for improvements. You have presented key assessment information to all members of the team. This has facilitated the cohesive approach to the effective delivery and assessment of the learners. This is demonstrated in the learners' excellent achievement. I have worked very effectively with you and found you to be a true professional. Targets/Action
Domain F Supporting access and progression	Achievements Very good support offered. This is demonstrated in exit routes. Targets/Action

Minimum Core	
Minimum core	Achievements You have successfully completed the minimum core. You have taught a wide range of learners, including a linguistically and culturally diverse group. Targets/Action To continue to develop inclusive resources.
Comments You have been very proactive in developing your approach to meeting the needs of a wide range of learners. You have used language-acquisition exercises to deconstruct the meta-language of law. This has proved to be an effective strategy in breaking down some real linguistic barriers. Further to this you have demonstrated a high level of ability in enhancing student general vocabulary alongside embedding the legal concepts.	

Summative feedback from supervising tutor

You have worked extremely hard this academic year to develop your practice and meet the needs of a wide range of learners. You have progressed from an interim grade of 2 to a summative grade of 1. This is because of your outstanding overall input into a well-established team, an input consisting of pastoral support for students, helping out with court and other visits, planning/administrative assistance to academic staff, attendance at board of studies. You have also been actively involved in discussions on curricular change and development.

Further to this you have completed all the academic assignments to deadlines and received very good feedback.

While on the programme you have taken the role of student rep and ambassador, carrying these out to a high level. You have been an excellent trainee with 100 per cent attendance both at university and on placement.

Trainee's reflection and evaluation on feedback

I am obviously very pleased to receive this feedback on triangulation. I feel that my participation in the PCET PGCE has enabled me to develop my practice in a profound way which has benefited the learners whom I have taught during my professional placement. This has undoubtedly been facilitated by the clear encouragement, support and professionalism shown by placement managers, the placement course team and, in particular, my subject-specific mentor. In addition, I have benefited from the invaluable support and encouragement of my personal tutor. I hope that in addition to benefiting learners, I have discharged my professional duty to my colleagues on placement.

To the future

Communities of practice

Once you have qualified and secured a teaching position you may want to continue actively to share the ideas and thoughts which have been provoked by this book. As busy practitioners finding the time to do this effectively can sometimes prove difficult. However, moving from the assumption that learning is something we do alone and instead joining a 'community of practice' can facilitate you actively to engage in meaningful dialogue with others in your specialised field. This dialogue involves more than the technical knowledge or skill associated with undertaking teaching; it offers you the opportunity to be actively involved in a set of relationships over time (Lave and Wenger, 1991, p98). The communities which grow from this have an impact on your personal and professional development and that of your learners.

You may want to visit the following sites of communities of practice.

Dialogue North West
www.lancs.ac.uk/dialogue_nw/index.htm
The aim of Dialogue North West is to create a forum where individuals and organisations in the northwest of England can share and develop research and practice in adult literacy, numeracy and ESOL. In doing this, it encourages the development of research by establishing networks and circulating information. The research forum encourages practitioners, providers, policymakers and researchers to take part in discussion, seminars, professional development opportunities and training events. The Dialogue North West steering group is made up of a diverse range of individuals and organisations involved in the Learning and Skills Sector, and the group is co-ordinated by the Lancaster Literacy Research Centre.

Research and Practice in Adult Literacy
www.literacy.lancs.ac.uk/rapal/
RaPAL is the only national organisation that focuses on the role of literacy in adult life in Britain. It campaigns for the rights of all adults to have access to the full range of literacies in their lives. It offers a critique of current policy and practice where it is based on simplistic notions of literacy as a skill. It argues for broader ideas of literacy starting from theories of language and literacy acquisition that take account of social context. The theories drawn on are broadly known as the new literacy studies.

RaPAL encourages a broad range of collaborative and reflective research involving all participants in literacy work as partners. It supports democratic practices in adult literacy work and believes that a learning democracy can only be achieved if teaching, learning and research are kept together. A dynamic relationship between research and practice keeps the meaning of literacy open and responsive to the variety of changing social contexts and practices that exist in our society.

Learning and Skills Research Network
www.lsrn.org.uk/
The Learning and Skills Research Network (LSRN) began in 1997 and was supported by the Learning and Skills Development Agency. It entered a new phase in April 2006 working collaboratively with multiple partner organisations. It is a network based in the regions of England and Northern Ireland. It brings together people involved in producing and making

use of research in the Learning and Skills Sector and higher education and provides a welcoming atmosphere for those new to research.

REFERENCE REFERENCE REFERENCE **REFERENCE** REFERENCE REFERENCE

Jean Lave and Eatienne Wenger (1991) *Situated Learning. Legitimate peripheral participation*. Cambridge: University of Cambridge Press.

Please contact me to share your stories of the impact of joining communities of practice: vicky.duckworth@edgehill.ac.uk